Endorsements

"I spent a delightful weekend reading…I highly recommend this little book to anyone aspiring to advance their career. The authors offer many practical ideas for influencing others using certain simple communication principles."

—Arthur C. Nielsen, Jr., Chairman Emeritus
A.C. Nielsen Co.

"After 40 years in the computerized information business, I know that this practical guide to career advancement is a winner, and long overdue."

—Robert A. Yellowlees
Retired Chairman and CEO
National Data Corporation

"I wish I had written this book myself! E-mail communication takes up a big part of every workday, and the 'bottom line' techniques outlined in this book certainly can help reduce the time spent in composing, reading and responding to e-mails. This is essential reading for anyone involved in the business world."

—Edwin R. Massey, Ph.D., President
Indian River Community College

About the Authors

John S. Fielden, Ph.D., University Professor Emeritus, was the Dean of the business schools at Boston University and the University of Alabama. He has been an Associate Editor of *The Harvard Business Review*, and a writing consultant to IBM, Kimberly-Clark, General Electric, Dun and Bradstreet, General Foods, and South Central Bell. He has authored nine *Harvard Business Review* articles, including the *HBR* classic, "What Do You Mean I Can't Write?" and several best-selling texts on business writing. Dr. Fielden and Dr. Dulek have been credited with popularizing the term *"Bottom Lining"* in reference to communications.

Jean D. Gibbons, Ph.D., Russell Professor Emerita, was the Chair of the Applied Statistics Program at the University of Alabama and Associate Professor at The Wharton School of Finance and Commerce. She is a Fellow of the American Statistical Association and the International Statistical Institute. She has published nine books on statistical methods for decision making and has been a consultant to South Central Bell and the United States Department of Defense. Her articles have appeared in the *Journal of the American Statistical Association, Journal of the Royal Statistical Society, and Technometrics*, among others.

Ronald E. Dulek, Ph.D. is the John R. Miller Professor of Management and Chair of the Department of Management and Marketing at the University of Alabama. He is a consultant to IBM, OSHA, the United States Department of Health and Human Services, AT & T, Sony, and other public and private organizations. His articles on business communications have been published in *Business Horizons, Journal of Business Communication, Personnel Journal, Personnel* magazine, and *IEEE Transactions on Professional Communications*.

Throw Me the Bottom Line...

I'm Drowning in E-mail!

Bob's Rules for
Managing the E-mail Crisis

John S. Fielden, Ph.D.
Jean D. Gibbons, Ph.D.
Ronald E. Dulek, Ph.D.

Pioneer River Press
Fort Pierce, Florida
©2003

ISBN 0-9745098-0-9

Printed in the United States of America

Published by
Pioneer River Press
3209 Virginia Avenue
Fort Pierce, FL 34981-5596
772.462.4786
772.462.4602 (fax)
http://www.PioneerRiver.com

Cover design by Jennifer Fleming, Indian River Community College

Dedication

We dedicate this book to the Indian River Community College Foundation in Fort Pierce, Florida, which has provided scholarships to thousands of deserving students who would not otherwise have been able to attend college.

We are pleased to contribute all proceeds from the sale of this book directly to the IRCC Foundation to be used in the areas of student, instructional, and facility support to provide better access and opportunities for students to continue their education. Many schools have slogans. But IRCC lives up to its slogan "Where the student is the most important person on campus!" in a sincere and effective way.

It has been a pleasure to work with the College and its Foundation. We thank Dr. Edwin R. Massey, IRCC President, and Jimmie Anne Haisley, Executive Director of the IRCC Foundation, for their strong leadership and courage to explore the art of communication. Our sincere thanks also go to Margot Barker, Jennifer Fleming, Melanie Forget, Patricia Profeta, and Denise Robinson for their enthusiasm and dedication to making this book a reality.

John S. Fielden, Ph.D.
Jean D. Gibbons, Ph.D.
Ronald E. Dulek, Ph.D.

Table of Contents

Acknowledgments

The authors generously offered the proceeds of this book to Indian River Community College (IRCC) because of its strong commitment to excellence and the fact that it lives up to its motto "Where the student is the most important person on campus!" The authors were excited to provide this entrepreneurial approach to raising funds to provide students with greater opportunities to receive a college education. Because the contents of this book align perfectly with the mission of the College and because the IRCC Foundation is always looking for creative and meaningful ways to provide additional avenues of support to students, the Foundation eagerly accepted the manuscript.

This venture provided the IRCC Foundation staff with the opportunity to work hand in hand with Dr. Jack Fielden and Dr. Jean Gibbons Fielden. We all enjoyed the brainstorming sessions and teamwork that took place to produce the final copy of this book. It was heartwarming to experience the enthusiasm that the Fieldens have about our institution. The principles in this book have markedly streamlined communication within the IRCC Foundation office.

IRCC is a comprehensive community college serving 40,000 students a year in the communities of Indian River, Martin, Okeechobee and St. Lucie counties on the east coast of Florida. IRCC prepares students for transfer to four-year universities and provides two-year degrees that prepare students to immediately enter the workforce.

For over a decade, IRCC students have typically achieved 100% on state and national licensure exams and have earned top passing scores on required State of Florida academic skills tests. In 2003, the Southern Association of Colleges and Schools (SACS) gave IRCC a nearly perfect accreditation review. Student learning is a top priority at IRCC, where 75.4% of state revenues go directly into instructional costs, the highest percentage in the state.

IRCC Foundation

FOREWORD:
Effective Communication is Timeless

Obviously, ours is the age of instantaneous electronic communications. Without e-mail, voice mail, or teleconferencing, big business today simply could not keep up the pace with which timely information must be exchanged. Yet all we hear are complaints that we are drowning in a flood of poorly written, rambling, often extraneous e-mail messages pouring in on us daily. What is the cause?

Bob knew the answer long ago. He saw the flood coming. He recognized that the speed and "easyness" of e-mail would prove to be destructive. Because it now is so incredibly simple for people to "copy" anyone who might just possibly have even a remote interest in a given subject, they do so and clutter up our in-boxes with time-wasting irrelevancies.

He also predicted that people who used to spend hours planning a detailed report on a complex subject would, in the new e-mail world, end up writing first and thinking later, if at all, about how the report should have been more logically organized.

"The fault, Dear Brutus," lies not with electronic equipment; it lies with all of us. WE have to learn how to write efficient, effective messages — no electronic wizardry can do that for us. Nor can such wizardry alter the fact that we are we are writing to sensitive people and not to machines, to people with feelings that can be hurt, to people who can not be given orders and need to be persuaded to do what is asked of them.

This is the book for you, for someone who is sincerely interested in getting ahead in a business world badly in need of people who know how to write economically, concisely, accurately, sensitively, and persuasively — and who do so only when writing serves a decidedly useful purpose.

Introduction

It's a Flood Out There! Can't You Stop it? Please!

The day we knew we HAD to write this book was January 10, 2002, when a headline in *The Wall Street Journal* caught our eye and reminded us of a commitment we had made to Bob, our mentor, many years ago. That headline warned readers that *"A Rising Flood of Office E-mail Messages Threatens to Drown the Unorganized."* The article (by Elizabeth Weinstein) told how top managers were seriously concerned about the costs incurred as a result of the time employees (including themselves) spend in writing and reading e-mails. The article quoted:

--- a mind-boggling estimate by International Data Corporation that 1.4 TRILLION e-mail messages were sent from U.S. businesses alone in 2001!

--- another research firm's calculation that the "average office worker spends 49 minutes a day on e-mail."

--- yet another research firm's estimate that "about four hours a day" were being spent on e-mail by top management!

Clearly, the day that Bob had predicted would surely come had indeed finally arrived — and, seemingly, with bells on! We all too vividly remembered the promise that we had made to Bob many years ago, when our long consulting job for him had finally, but amicably, concluded.

Bob had thrown us a very teary and slightly liquid farewell party. At the party's conclusion, Bob rose. "You guys," he said, lifting a glass, "are a tad younger than I am. So I'm going to pass on to you a serious concern I have about business writing in the future. My worry is about electronic mail. Its use is spreading fast from the technical personnel in our labs and factories to people in our business offices. Based on what I've seen of this writing, most of it is poorly organized, just thoughts meandering across the screen with no logical organization. And much of it is borderline illiterate. I can't understand how college graduates can write so poorly. And above all," he said, shaking his head sadly, "they don't bottom line it!"

He drew a deep breath and continued. "I don't know how far this electronic mail thing is going to spread in everyday business use. But if it does spread, things will be worse than they were when I first brought you guys in. More people will be able to waste more time of more other people faster and more completely than at any time in man's history."

Bob's last words to us were these: "But if it does spread and not improve in quality in the future, I want you to swear that you will declare war on ineffectual, time-wasting writing, just as I did."

* * * * * * * * * * * *

In our mind's eye now, years later, it was pretty easy to imagine Bob sitting at the big desk in his office, waving this *Wall Street Journal* article at us and demanding to know, in his usual peremptory tone, "What are you going to do about this situation?" He would scold, "Well, don't just sit there. You made me a promise and I am holding you to it. So, what are you going to do?"

"What do you mean, what are we going to do? How in the world can we declare war on a flood of messages?" We scoffed at the notion.

"Come on, now," Bob certainly would have responded. "You're not dumb. This is right up your alley. Bad writing is what's causing the flood. You know perfectly well that this flood is fed by the simple fact that people are writing so poorly, so vaguely that, many more times than not, single messages fail to do the job. People have to write back and ask, 'What did your last memo mean?' or 'Just tell me what you want me to do and I'll be happy to do it.' One message becomes three…that is, if the original writer succeeds in accomplishing in a second message what he or she failed to do in the first.

"It's the same old story. People tend to get an idea in their heads and then succumb to an irresistible urge to broadcast it, with the flick of their finger, to a bunch of readers, many of whom have no possible use for, or even interest in, what they have just received. It's really the identical problem that you and I addressed years ago. Nothing is really different about writing in this e-mail era, other than its capacity for allowing people to fire off multiple copies of nothing to lots of people.

"But in terms of what makes written messages *intrinsically* efficient, economical, and effective, there's no difference between then and now. It's still basically a matter of how clearly something is expressed, and how relevant it is to a reader's interests and concerns. What possible difference does it make in the quality and effectiveness of communications if people write letters on computers instead of typewriters? What difference would it make, for that matter, if they wrote them in pen and ink, or on papyrus, or on clay tablets?

"The big difference between then and now is this. The modern business writing era is a communications free-for-all. It's like an unsupervised tag-team match. You can write to whomever you like, whenever you like. No one judges WHAT you write, HOW WELL you write it, HOW MUCH you can write, or HOW OFTEN you can write.

"Look at what today's top executives are crying about!" Our imagined Bob was waving the *Journal* article under our noses again. "Not a tear is shed about the quality of the writing they get, but only about the fact that it comes in floods. They must be taking stupid pills. It is blatantly obvious that this flood is the cumulative result of writers not knowing how to bottom line what they write. Not knowing how to be coherent and well organized. Letting their thoughts just wander all over the place. Moreover, nobody's evidently ever heard of my 'So What?' test.

"The result is this nationwide flood of poorly written twaddle, which is wasting everyone's time and energy. And don't overlook the cost. For the cost of time spent writing each piece of drivel, there is another cost for time spent in reading the drivel."

Bob fixed us with one of his more baleful glares. "So far as I can tell, you have just been sitting around, doing nothing about all this. Get off your butts and keep your promise to me. Give these top executives something valuable to use to fight against this flood of bad writing!

"You know my Rules, backward and forward. Share them! I don't have to tell you to blow the dust off them, for there is no dust on them. They are just as relevant and needed today as they were years ago. And they will be just as relevant and valuable at any time in the future. Rules for clear, economical, time- and money-saving writing will never go out of style.

"You've still got all the teaching materials we developed in our company. So, round up your troop of flood busters! Make war on one more flood in your lifetime! You <u>can</u> do it and you <u>should</u> do it! And, by God, you <u>will</u> do it, or I'll know the reason why!"

* * * * * * * * * * *

Needless to say, this book is our way of keeping that promise to Bob.

Bob's War on the Flood

Putting a Finger in the Dike

When we first met the real life Bob, he was the Executive Vice President of the largest division of an extremely large and successful international corporation. He was a bit older than we were, far better looking, and a hell of a lot more obsessed with good business writing than we were, even though we had taught the subject and had written some pretty well-received articles on the topic.

Bob sent two assistants and a corporate jet to pick us up and deliver us to a meeting with him at his divisional headquarters. The more talkative assistant told us the boss had seen some articles we had written on business writing, liked them, and wanted to talk with us.

As soon as we entered his office, he told us in an agitated voice that he was "fed up" and that he was "declaring war on bad writing" in his company, and that we were to do the fighting. We started to reply, but he stopped us with an upturned palm. "Do you guys have any idea how much time each of us in management spends reading and rereading memos that might POSSIBLY, and I mean POSSIBLY, contain some cleverly hidden information we actually need to know?"

We shook our heads. "Too damn much," he answered. "I'm sick and tired of having to wade through every memo or report I get, trying to find the bottom line!"

"Find the WHAT?" we asked.

"The Bottom Line! I want to know why I'm being written to! I want to know what they want of me. And I want to know damn quick! I'm busy!"

Thus was the term "bottom lining" stolen from the field of finance and applied to writing. We snapped it up and used it not only in the instructional programs we gave for the various divisions of Bob's corporation but, over the years, in articles and textbooks that we wrote. We even got written up in an article about bottom lining featured in *USA Today* (August 10, 1984). Business people loved the term. English teachers hated it. "Bottom lining? Too vulgar! Too businessy!" they complained. We let them rave.

Bob hired us as mercenaries in his war on bad writing. That was long ago. Bottom lining, the "science" of efficient writing, has long been forgotten, as the e-mail we get daily proves convincingly. Do people today need to know how to bottom line (BL)? You bet they do! And more than ever today.

* * * * * * * * * * *

Bob's cure for the problem facing him and his divisional managers was for us to train his people to "stop beating around the damn bush!" We asked for samples of some of the memos and reports he disliked. Bob rummaged through a pile of papers on his desk, glared at one of them and handed it to us. "Look at this beauty!" he said. "And it's one of the short ones." Here is the copy of that un-memorable memorandum:

To: Bob
From: Staff Assistant
Subject: Consolidation of Marketing Functions in New Office Facilities

I am working with our organization department on consolidating headquarters marketing functions into the new building at Pebble Brook. The new building will be ready for occupancy in September.

I recommend the following occupancy plan for the Pebble Brook building:

1. *Consolidate all of the Marketing Communications people into this new building.*
2. *Relocate our Advertising and Media people from Northside to this new building.*
3. *Leave Market Research in its current location but provide it with additional space for expansion.*
4. *Centralize the Procurement function entirely in the new building.*

These moves will consolidate all of headquarters Marketing into the Pebble Brook location with the exception of people in Marketing Research. They will remain in Building A because of their heavy utilization of our computer facilities.

I have attached a preliminary building layout, floor by floor. Please let me know if you agree with this plan.

"What do you think of it?" Bob snapped, fixing us with a glare.

"Well, at least it's short," we replied.

"Short? What's short got to do with it?" Bob was exasperated. "Shortness isn't everything! Shortness is not the point. The point is that until the last sentence of this memo, this guy's been wasting my time. I read his four points, all the while wondering why is he telling me all this? I want to know what's the BL!

"You guys don't understand what in the hell I'm getting at. You don't know what a BL is! For heaven's sakes, look at this guy's last sentence. Really look at it! What does he say to me? 'Please let me know if you agree with this plan.' Don't you realize that this last sentence is the BL? That's a swell time to tell me what he wants of me. After I've waded through his four points, wondering why in the world he is telling me all this! Then, and only then, does he tell me what he should have told me in the very first sentence. That I'm supposed to judge the damned plan! Now I have to go back to the beginning to see if I want to approve the plan or not. I have to read the damn memo TWICE! If he had told me the BL first, I could have made my judgment on the first reading.

"Can you imagine how many hundreds of thousands of memos, letters, and reports are written yearly in a corporation the size of this one? And among those thousands of memos, what percent are bottom lined? No more than ten percent, I'd bet. It's gotten so bad that most of us have to just about stand on our heads to read the memos we get. That way we can read the last sentence or paragraph first and find out right away what the devil they want of us. And that's only when they haven't buried the bottom line somewhere in the middle of the next-to-last paragraph, or forgotten to put a bottom line in at all."

Bob pointed his finger at us accusingly. "You guys think I'm just being picky. You can't grasp the enormity of the fact that this memo is typical. I'm not fooling. And every person writing or reading these thousands of time-wasting pieces of writing gets a salary. So I'm talking about gazillions of dollars here, not peanuts!"

Bob looked at his watch. "Got a meeting," he grunted. "I want you guys to fix things. I'm counting on you to clean this up. I'm sick of it!" On his way out the door, he shouted back at us, "See my secretary. She'll arrange to have you sent a ton of sample memos and reports from all over the company. Read them! Then you'll have some appreciation of how I have to suffer!"

About two weeks later, we received a large cardboard carton. Over the next two weeks, we read through, if not a ton, then at least several hundred pounds of the enclosed memos, letters and reports. From an English teacher's point of view, they didn't look bad. Meticulous punctuation, spelling, paragraphing and all the niceties that skilled secretaries and word processing centers could contribute. But we could see, from Bob's point of view, nine out of ten were, in fact, organized upside down and many never made clear what they wanted of their reader. We phoned Bob and told him we were ready to talk.

Two days later, we were once again in Bob's office. "Enjoy reading all that stuff?" he asked. We answered that we could see his point, that most of the memos didn't begin well. "Begin well?" he snapped. "I knew you'd say something silly like that! It's my fault for letting you go away with the notion that the principle of BLing applies only to the first sentence or two of a memo. That's only the start of where it applies.

"You've got to recognize that writing in the business environment is a constant contest between writers and readers. We're all busy — very

8

busy. Reading the crap that crosses our desks every day takes up valuable time we could use doing something useful," he snickered, "like answering the crap we received yesterday. You get so you hate to read. Consequently, writers have to blast their way into the readers' minds, make an impact on them, make it perfectly clear why they should pay attention to what you're telling them.

"Sure, the first line is critical. If the writer doesn't immediately tell you why you should read the message, why should you spend time trying to figure it out? You've got better things to do. But BLing must be applied to every part of what you write. BLing is really about the psychological organization of thoughts, expressed in words." Bob stopped and looked pleased with himself. "You know, I've never said that before. But that's exactly what it is. The right words. The right sentences. The right paragraphs. Presented in the most logical way possible.

"That's why I need you guys. I know exactly what I want, and what it takes to dramatically improve communications in this company; but I don't have time to do anything about it. I don't have time to spend developing teaching materials, let alone actually teaching all the people who need help in this company. That's what you've got to do for me. That's why I've brought you guys in. I'll work with you as much as I can."

We did as we were instructed. Our job was to create programs on BL beginnings, BL sentences, BL paragraphs and, impossible though it seemed, BL long reports.

Throw Me the Bottom Line...I'm Drowning in E-Mail!

Bob's "So What?" Test

Why Me? What Did I Do to Deserve This?

Our training sessions began with a staggered schedule. As soon as we had accumulated enough Bob-approved material to keep a class profitably working for half a day, we informed Bob and he pushed the necessary buttons and classes were formally scheduled.

The first classes were devoted to BLing the first sentence of any communication. The participants (trainees) all were recent college graduates, mostly in business and engineering, ranging in age from the middle twenties to the very early thirties. Some were various sorts of staff assistants, and some of the more experienced were administrative assistants to middle managers in Bob's division. We were surprised to find that a group of such high quality personnel had serious problems in identifying the BL in the sample memos we had collected. The reason was that true BL opening sentences rarely appeared first, but instead were buried somewhere in the body of the memo.

The trainees blamed anything they didn't like about a memo on the unknown — and obviously untalented — author of any memo that came under discussion. In order to knock down this defense, we asked them to bring in copies of memos they themselves had written. Of course, being no fools, they showed up with what they believed to be their best efforts.

11

It did them no good. Trainees had real difficulty pointing out BL sentences even in their own memos because they were invariably hidden in the middle of the third or fourth paragraph! Bob was right. They simply had no understanding of the concept of BLing. We had to find a way to teach them how to distinguish between BL and non-BL opening sentences.

We found that the most effective way for people to tell a BL from a non-BL opening sentence was to apply what Bob called his "So What?" test. To apply this test, ask yourself, "So what is this to me?" Or, "Why in the world are you telling ME this?" after reading each of the following three sample opening sentences. Assume that each is the first sentence of an unsolicited memo sent to you. Also assume that you have not requested the information conveyed in each. Which sentence, if any, passes your "So What?" test:

Test Group

A. *The proposal from the XYZ company arrived Thursday.*

B. *It is evident that employees in many areas of our operations will need technical retraining.*

C. *Mary Gobel represented us at the semi-annual meeting of the Fire Safety Committee.*

We feel sure that your answer is "None!" Each deserves being greeted with a rousing "So What?" Now let's rewrite these sentences so that they immediately make clear why this information is being told to you:

A. *Enclosed is XYZ's new proposal which we are prepared to accept, unless you register immediately strong and convincing objections.*

B. *Please make sure that the following employees in your operation are signed up for technical retraining.*

C. *Mary Gobel, our representative to the Fire Safety Task Force, reports that we are in full compliance with all fire safety standards and need take no remedial steps.*

Now let's see if the "So What?" test can help you distinguish which, if any, of the following nine opening sentences expresses the BL of these messages. Remember, you are to assume that each is the *first* sentence of an unsolicited memo sent to you. Don't worry about rewriting them. Just decide which are BL and which are not.

OPENING SENTENCES

1. *As you are probably aware, this office is required to make a yearly report on the results of our right-of-way negotiations.*

2. *I need to have you tell me the number of parcels acquired per professional grade employee as well as the percent of tracts condemned.*

3. *We realize that you have no right-of-way work assigned other than nominal value signs.*

4. *The financial coordinator is responsible for five separate activities.*

5. *Only Legal is authorized to seek and acquire permission for building improvements.*

6. *Since it is highly probable that our new policy on standardizing parts nomenclature will affect your operation, here is an explanation of why this policy was adopted and the long-range benefits it promises.*

7. *Materials costs now comprise 40% of the sales value of our products.*

8. *Some companies have proposed combining Production, Control, Purchasing, and Distribution into a single Materials Management department.*

9. *Please ask your staff to conduct an in-depth evaluation of our current materials organization and recommend any changes that might improve our ability to control materials costs.*

(The correct answers are given at the end of the next chapter.)

Throw Me the Bottom Line...I'm Drowning in E-Mail!

Bob on High Impact Writing

Flood Surges Make Big Waves

Something we had said about good writing, apparently at our last meeting with Bob, had stuck in his craw, for he greeted us with the first of many desk-pounding, finger-pointing, arm-waving scoldings we were to receive over the years. "Listen," he shouted, as soon as we entered his office, "don't start teaching GOOD writing from an English teacher's point of view. It's not about some would-be Hemingway trying to write the great American novel and throwing away the first ten drafts. This is business and everybody's busy. Someone's always after someone else to get something done. And there's never enough time.

"Every writer is competing with every other writer for the reader's attention. So what you write has to virtually leap off the page at the reader. It's got to be delivered in a high-impact way in order to muscle your message to the head of the line, out in front of all the other 'must-do' things already on the reader's mind, and demand his or her attention! BLing your subject is just the beginning. Every sentence, every paragraph must jump off the page into the reader's mind.

"Over the weekend, I worked up some before-and-after examples to make sure you understand exactly what I mean by high-impact." Here is the first example Bob gave us:

Example A. (Original): The key point is that all too few companies possess a fully integrated scheme for breaking down corporate objectives into man-size chunks, establishing individual performance standards, establishing wage, salary and employee benefit structures, appraising performance at regular intervals, and rewarding, or taking remedial steps, on the basis of active performance.

Bob pointed out, "This example makes zero impact on a busy reader. One glance at this glob of information and the reader is immediately turned off. Here's how I'd make it high-impact:"

Example A. (Revised): The key point is that all too few companies possess a fully integrated scheme for:

1. *Breaking down corporate objectives into man-size chunks,*
2. *Establishing individual performance standards,*
3. *Gaining acceptance of performance standards,*
4. *Establishing wage, salary, and employee benefits packages,*
5. *Appraising performance at regular intervals, and*
6. *Rewarding, or taking remedial steps, on the basis of actual performance.*

Bob looked at us questioningly. "I suppose you think that all I did was put things into a list. Sure, that's just what I did. But in doing so, I presented information in exactly the way the mind stores information — not in one big glob, but in small bites, easier to swallow. What did you do when you were in school? Didn't you boil your notes down just before a test? Didn't you make lists of everything you wanted to memorize? Sure you did. So why not present difficult-to-remember information in an easier-to-remember fashion in the first place?"

We said nothing. "Something bothering you?" Bob asked.

"No, there's nothing wrong with listing the points. Makes it much easier to comprehend."

"So?"

We bit the bullet for the first of many, many times with Bob. "It's just that the first sentence of your revised list is not the BL. It doesn't pass your 'So What?' test."

Instead of being angry, Bob was delighted. "Hey, that's good! Give the trainees the low-impact version and ask them not only to high-impact it, but also to put in a BL statement in front of the lists that will pass the 'So What?' test. Let me see...something like this might do it." Here is what he showed us:

Example A. (Revised for High Impact and BLed): I want your committee to begin immediate development of a fully integrated personnel appraisal and reward scheme, something all too few companies have, and which we need. This scheme must include specific steps for: [items 1 through 6 are then listed.]

Here's another example Bob worked out for us:

Example B. (Original): The customer utilizing repair center maintenance is responsible for determining when remedial maintenance is required, for removing and replacing machines in the operational environment, for checking machine performance while machines are installed in the operational environment, for shipping machines prepaid to our repair center, and for utilizing designated containers available from us for such shipment.

Example B. (Revised for High Impact but not BLed): The customer utilizing repair center maintenance is responsible for:

1. *Determining when remedial maintenance is required,*
2. *Removing and replacing machines in the operational environment,*
3. *Checking machine performance while machines are installed in the operational environment,*
4. *Shipping machines prepaid to our repair centers, and*
5. *Utilizing designated containers available from us for each shipment.*

"How would I add a BL to this?" Bob wondered. He thought for a moment, then said, "Got it! Simple enough. The BL opening sentence should read something like this:

Example B. (Revised for High Impact and BLed): You are personally responsible for making certain that all of your customers are apprised in writing of their responsibilities when they make use of repair center maintenance. They are specifically responsible for: [Then 1, 2, 3, 4 and 5 are listed.]

We nodded. "That ought to do it. Thanks."

**[The answers that pass Bob's "So What?" Test
are sentences 2, 6, and 9.]**

Bob on Coherent Bricklaying

Brick By Brick, We're Building a Life Raft

We happened to poke our noses into Bob's office one day. His secretary whispered, "He's in a bad mood today." "Something he read?" we guessed. "Right on the nose," she replied.

Bob was a man not easily pleased by anything he had to read. But he was especially annoyed by vague, incoherent writing that resulted from poor organization of thoughts. Such was the case at the moment. As soon as he laid eyes on us, he shouted, "If most of the people who write to me were bricklayers, they'd be doing little more than dumping their load of bricks onto a page and telling me: 'You sort it out, wise guy. You make sense of it.'" He smacked his hand on the desk. "I don't like this at all. It's wasting my time. It's wasting company money. Do something about it!"

"You mean, teach coherence?" we asked, fearing the worst.

"Whatever," Bob replied, with a shrug. "Call it what you will. But I call it bricklaying. Just teach them how to lay word bricks in an orderly fashion. It's all part of BLing, isn't it? Getting thoughts organized so they are easily and quickly understood? Just fix it!" He dismissed us with an airy wave of his hand.

"Fix it? Where do we begin?" we thought. We were stumped. The smallest units of writing, of course, were words and sentences. We

19

shrugged off any consideration of spending time teaching apt word choice. After all, these people were not aspiring to be poets. So we focused on sentences, facing up to the fact that in order to teach BLing, we had to teach sentence structure, because that was where BLing begins.

But teaching BL sentence structure to a bunch of business school grads was not going to be a picnic. We felt sure that they would remember little or nothing from their freshman composition course — certainly little about formal grammar, and even less about the diagramming of sentences. And some form of this was exactly what we had to do in order to teach the nuts and bolts of BLing. But how could we diagram sentences without boring the socks off our trainees in the process? Fortunately, Bob, quite accidentally, came to our rescue. Here is how this miracle happened.

Bob's mind was the epitome of the business mind. SIMPLIFY, SIMPLIFY was one of his favorite mantras. To him, everything in writing was a "brick" — words, sentences, paragraphs, sections of a report, chapters in a book. They all had to be sequenced in an absolutely logical BL order, with the most important coming first. No excuses! To our amazement, Bob's bricklaying metaphor proved to be very "teachable" with the future business leaders we faced in our classes.

Effective writers, perhaps unconsciously, have the knack of arranging related words, phrases, clauses, gerunds, participles, etc. (no wonder Bob called them "bricks"!) in their minds before putting them in writing. By contrast, weak writers take their bricks and just dump them in a confusing jumble and expect the reader to rearrange them so as to make sense. Bob was right, there were three types of "brick" problems we frequently found in various writings in Bob's company:

1. Misplaced bricks.
2. Dangling bricks.
3. Vague pronoun bricks.

MISPLACED BRICKS

Errors involving misplaced bricks are by far the most common, probably because they result from people not taking a hard look at what they have ACTUALLY written, as opposed to what they MEANT to write. Take a look at this simple example:

"Profits will never save the company, if kept at a minimum."

In Bob's terms, here are two bricks, separated by a comma. (For those who might actually care, brick 1 is an independent clause; in other words, a complete subject-verb-object sentence. Brick 2 is a modifying phrase — a phrase because it is not a complete sentence, and modifying because it adds to, or alters the meaning of brick 1.) Now, just ask yourself, WHAT, according to this writer, is "being kept at a minimum"?

As written, it is the "company" that is being kept at a minimum. Common sense tells us that the writer meant this phrase to modify and hence refer to the brick about "Profits." So what did you, as the reader, have to do to make sense of the original? You had to move the bricks around logically, as the writer should have done; i.e., "Profits, if kept at a minimum, will never save the company." And every time you, as a reader, do something like this, you are doing the writer's work. And, like Bob, you resent it.

DANGLING BRICKS

Dangling bricks are far less common than misplaced bricks. But they tend to occur in important documents, where clarity is critical. And they are often impossible for the reader to fix. Readers are completely stumped when they attempt to make sense of a sentence where the critical brick is nowhere to be found in it. For example:

"After deciding on a course of action, the best strategy seemed to be to buy, not make, the components."

After your mind divides the sentence into bricks, it asks, "WHO is deciding on a course of action?" Certainly not the "best strategy." The "after deciding" brick modifies (or refers) to a mysterious "decider" who the writer has not bothered to insert into the sentence. This type of vague

21

statement cannot be corrected by readers who have no idea who the secret decider is. Consequently, such mistakes tend to show up in instances where the writer's vagueness is intentional and self-serving, rather than an error. Bob hated this type of evasion of responsibility with a passion.

VAGUE PRONOUN BRICKS

Bob also hated vague pronouns. "HE said? Who in the devil is HE?" Bob would yell. He instructed us to teach our trainees to avoid pronouns as much as possible. "Pronouns are tricky!" he claimed. He gave us an example to use in our classes where his company (call it Company A) was in a legal wrangle with Company B. The dispute centered around who was to pay certain costs. The following paragraph was the critical part of a document which had been entered into evidence in a civil suit.

> *A summation of a recent dispute between Company A and Company B shows that their management had responsibility for transmitting to customers all relevant costs to be expected in installing the system in question. They had no authority to the contrary, and they should have understood that incidental costs would be charged to them. They were instead vague.*

The whole issue revolved around the answer to this question: "Which company is the 'THEY'? Who owes the money? A or B?"

Pronouns are bricks which mean nothing unless there is another brick which clarifies who or what the pronoun refers to. Bob's advice was: "Avoid pronouns as much as possible. And use none at all in documents that are important and possibly litigious." Undoubtedly, tricky pronouns are why lawyers use such stilted language as "the party of the first part," or "the party of the second part." They make sure that page one of their document identifies exactly who each of the parties is, "first party" or "second party," and that vague pronoun references never occur.

Bottom Lining Long Reports

Hold Your Breath — We're Diving to the Bottom!

Bob's job required that he "wade through" long, complicated reports from time to time. He hated it. So, as usual, he called us in and told us to teach trainees how to BL a ten or twenty page report. "What is wrong with the reports I read is what's been wrong with shorter forms of writing," he told us, "only long reports are more of a pain in the butt to read and undoubtedly more of a pain to write."

"Know what causes the trouble at both ends — the writing and the reading?" he asked. "Most of the people writing something even the slightest bit complicated have no good idea of what they really want to say until AFTER they've written it. Because of this, they end up giving me a report that is a chronological history of their thoughts as they worked their way through to a conclusion. And what I want, of course, is the conclusion first, then the justification."

"For example, suppose I ask someone to report to me about whether or not we should do business with Smith & Brown. Here's exactly the way most people would instinctively end up organizing their report:

This report deals with the question of whether we should do business with Smith and Brown. Here are my thoughts:

> a. *There are certain benefits to dealing with Smith & Brown. [These are listed at length.]*

b. There are certain disadvantages. *[These are also listed at length.]*

c. After weighing the advantages against the disadvantages, I conclude that the disadvantages outweigh the advantages. *[This discussion may also be lengthy.]*

d. Therefore, I recommend that we not do business with Smith & Brown.

"Three guesses where the BL showed up? At the end, of course. Why in the world can't they just say, 'I recommend that we not do business with Smith and Brown. Here is why:'?"

"Maybe," we speculated, "it's because so many of your people have engineering or other technical backgrounds. That's the way they've been trained to think and to write."

"Hell's bells!" Bob scoffed. "I know that. The old scientific method excuse! But they're not writing some scholarly paper, for Pete's sake! This is business, not some scientific laboratory where they have all the time in the world. They've got to learn to communicate as busy business people do. That's what business means — BUSY-NESS! — and don't you forget it!"

We told him we wouldn't. And to prove it, here is a distillation of all that Bob told us about how BL reports should be written to be more effective.

1. In a long report, the opening paragraph must tell the reader the BL — specifically, what the report's findings or recommendations are, and why this information should be of use to the reader.

Absolutely nothing ticked Bob off more than finding out, halfway through some lengthy disquisition, that the information, so painstakingly presented, was of no earthly use to him. Why did this happen so frequently? We speculated that it was because of Bob's position as Executive Vice President. As such, he had — or was thought to have — his fingers in many pies. Some subordinates, too many for Bob, drew the conclusion that he might, just might, want to know EVERYTHING happening in the division; so they played it "safe" by sending him reports on EVERYTHING! Undoubtedly, some sent him boring reports just to prove how hard they were working and how smart they were.

"I'm like a damn magnet!" he said. "If only you guys could teach them that it is ten to twenty times more important to BL a long report than it is to BL a memo. And the very beginning of a long report had damned well better be able to pass my 'So What?' test."

2. The report must tell the reader exactly how the report is organized — the sequence in which each topic is being presented. The writer must make sure that all sections of a long report follow exactly in the order promised. Bob called this "making a contract with the reader and then keeping it." Therefore, in our teaching we called this a "contract statement."

3. Long, complex reports require that each section must include a subcontract statement to serve as a "road map" for that section's discussion. The same applies to subsections. Contract statements not only aid readers; they also help writers by forcing them either to present exactly what their contract statement promises, or to go back and change the order of topics promised in the contract statement.

4. If a writer feels strongly (or really knows) that presenting BL conclusions or recommendations first will make absolutely no sense to the reader, and that the writer absolutely has to "educate" the reader thoroughly on the subject before presenting any recommendations, then the writer MUST tell the reader exactly that, and ask the reader's indulgence. "I have no objection to that," Bob said. "In fact, I'd rather the writer tell me up front that I'm too dumb to understand what he wants to tell me than force me to discover it for myself, ten pages and thirty minutes later!"

While Bob complained constantly about how much he hated reading long reports, neither he nor we could think of any additions to our training program that would help stem their flow toward his desk. Instead, we put heavy emphasis on BL organization of ideas so that ideas followed each other in long reports in the exact way promised by the writer. "At least," Bob said, "I won't waste so much time having to reassemble mentally a flock of pages full of bricks that make no sense in the order they've been left lying around."

As reinforcement to our teaching efforts, he sent to all department heads the following prototype as a sample of how any relatively long reports coming to him in the future from their department MUST begin:

TO: Bob
FROM: Anyone
SUBJECT: Recommendations regarding XYZ

[A subject line is NOT intended to take the place of the first sentence of your report. The first statement is where you MUST tell me why I am being given this information and what I'm supposed to do about it. If you cannot tell me why and what, please do not write to me. Here is how a very good report should begin.]

This report, as you requested, offers my analysis of XYZ's plant problems. It contains two sections. Section I deals with an immediate problem negatively affecting the plant's operation — high employee turnover. Section II deals with less urgent, long-run concerns — plant expansion and possible new products.

Here is a synopsis of the recommendations made for your consideration. We would like to hear whether you accept or reject these recommendations.

We recommend that immediate steps be taken to deal with employee turnover. Personnel turnover is 15% above average levels for similar employers in our area. The primary causes seem to be noncompetitive salaries, as well as low hourly wage rates, rather than working conditions. Wage and salary increases of 10 to 12% are recommended for your consideration.

We also recommend that any further serious study of possible plant expansion and possible new products be deferred until such time as the plant's immediate problems have been solved.

The reasons supporting these recommendations are explained fully in Sections I and II, respectively.

* * * * * * * * * * *

So far, we have covered all that Bob had taught us on BLing. Exhibit A, which follows, offers a summary of Bob's Bottom Line Rules which apply to 90 plus percent of all business writing. At this point, we thought we had been taught, and were teaching, everything that anyone needed to know about successful writing in the real world of business.

But we were wrong. We had a lot more to learn. For great as it is, efficient as it is, BLing can be highly dysfunctional, to say the least, when applied to some of the message types prevalent in the remaining 10% of business communications. The problem, as you will read in the pages ahead, is that BLing does not work at all well when we are dealing with messages that evoke strong negative emotional reactions in readers. That is where BLPLUS must take over, and that is what we deal with next.

EXHIBIT A. BOB'S RULES FOR BOTTOM LINING NONSENSITIVE MESSAGES

Rule 1. Immediately state your purpose for writing. Your first sentence must pass the reader's "So What?" test.

Rule 2. If you have more than one purpose for writing, state both purposes at the beginning of your memo. If doing this proves to be cumbersome or confusing, write two separate memos.

Rule 3. If you are making an action request of the reader, by all means BL it! Never bury an action request in the middle of a later paragraph. Readers may give up on you and stop reading before getting to the action request.

Rule 4. Present information in the order of its importance to your readers, not its importance to you.

Rule 5. If you think it necessary to include some information that may or may not be of importance to your reader, put it in an attachment.

Rule 6. Facilitate your readers' comprehension of your sentences by writing them in a simple, clear subject-verb-object order.

Rule 7. Lay out your thought "bricks" in strict logical order by putting ideas that relate to each other as close together as possible.

Rule 8. Avoid using pronouns as much as possible. When you do use them, recognize that pronouns mean nothing unless your reader knows exactly which noun the pronoun refers to. Therefore, always put the noun first and closely follow it with the appropriate pronoun.

Rule 9. If compound or complex sentences are necessary, always put the clause containing the most important thought first.

Rule 10. In complicated and/or long reports, make a contract with your reader as to the direction your discussion will be going. Regard this statement as a binding contract on your part. Fulfill every clause of that contract in the same sequence promised in your contract statement.

Rule 11. If your report has multiple sections, write a BL sentence for each subsection that tells the subject covered. And, if a particular subsection is complicated, write a contract statement for that section.

Enhancing the Bottom Line

Is "So What?" All that Matters?

Our BL classes had, just as Bob demanded, dramatically reduced the flood of bad, time-wasting writing in Bob's corporation. Bob was happy, we were happy, but our trainees were not — decidedly not.

We had taught BLing to our trainees as if they were writing in an emotional vacuum, as if readers of all business messages were devoid of feelings. We had also taught as if there were no distinct levels of power existing within corporations. Our classes were instructed to BL everything, regardless of the whether their readers were superiors or inferiors.

For years we had no trouble with BLing's assumption of a non-emotional, non-rank-conscious business world. But there came a time when telling trainees they must BL everything written to their bosses, even things the bosses wouldn't like to hear, we ended up actually getting booed.

We felt aggrieved. For years, we had diligently taught trainees what Bob had taught us — and for years, our students had lapped it up. That is, they did until it became obvious to everyone but Bob that BLing suffered from a significant shortcoming — not every boss was as open to criticism as Bob was. He was basically a very nice guy. He was tough, but he was fair. He could take hard truths as well as he could dish them out. He thought everyone was just like him. And in this he was wrong.

Many bosses can't take criticism, even when it is well meant, and constructive.

Consequently, we had a serious problem on our hands. Our trainees had formed the firm opinion that BLing, while great in principle most of the time, was not so hot when it came to the communication of something unpleasant or negative to their boss. It reflected their clear recognition that it was not rational to believe that communicating with one's superiors in a way that could even possibly be construed as blunt and terse, at best, and rude, insubordinate or even insulting, at worst, was not the smartest way to climb the corporate ladder. Everybody in his or her right mind, except Bob at the time, would have agreed with them.

Troubles began some months before, when a student in one of our classes told this anecdote. "Two years ago," she said, "I worked for a manager who demanded BLing. He gave me a draft of a marketing plan he was supposed to present to a high-level management committee. My boss was extremely proud of his plan. However, upon reading it, I felt, for various reasons, that it was way off target — so much so that presenting it to the committee, in its present form, was frankly a mistake. My boss had always assured me that he revered the truth and that I could always tell him what I honestly thought, without a qualm. So I told him he ought to ask for more time to work on his report, so that he could shore up some weak areas that I was foolish enough to enumerate."

"What happened?" the class asked. "He gave me the worst annual performance evaluation I ever received," she answered. "As a result, I am worse off today than I was two years ago."

This simple story was the kickoff for our troubles. This trainee's story was echoed by those of others who had been hurt as a result of BLing something their bosses did NOT want to hear. What we had at first assumed to be just a normal amount of griping about one's boss became serious — and by serious we mean that it was threatening our pocketbook.

At the completion of each several-week training session, trainees would fill out a performance evaluation, rating instructors on a 1 to 5 scale. A score of 5 was "excellent," and this was what the corporation fully expected each "outside" instructor to receive. Our scores, of late, had fallen down around our socks.

We knew there was no point in arguing, once more, with Bob about the wisdom, or lack thereof, of adhering to a firm rule that EVERYTHING must be BLed, even things quite painful or annoying to one's reader. In these arguments, Bob had never yet physically kicked us out of his office — even after the one time we lost our cool and told him exactly what his problem was. We told him that he did not appreciate the fact that 99% of what he wrote daily was to readers who were subservient to him, while 99% of what our trainees wrote was to readers who were definitely above them in rank.

No matter what arguments we offered, he flatly refused to admit that any of our trainees might have some justifiable reason for being leery of BLing negative messages to their bosses. He snickered; he scoffed. He rummaged through the usual pile of memos on his desk and proudly showed us an example of the way his administrative assistant BLed negative stuff to him:

To: Bob
From: Eileen

As you requested, I have carefully read your proposed report to the Planning Committee. I believe that the section dealing with possible new products is still somewhat vague. Perhaps the problem is with my lack of detailed knowledge of the topic. However, I felt I should bring this to your attention.

Bob glared at us. "So, what's there for me to get mad about?" he demanded. "I wanted her frank opinion and I got it."

We replied as tactfully as we could that perhaps his relationship with his assistant was different from that of many bosses with theirs. Bob shrugged and said, "I doubt it." That ended that. We had no choice but to continue, tails between our legs, to slog along to our classrooms, trying to become inured to the razzberries the trainees were giving us. Fortune was on our side, however. We got a lucky break because Bob had suddenly become obsessed with something other than BLing. His secretary called and suggested we go at once to his office. Naturally, we expected the worst. It turned out, however, that he had called us in to discuss a new problem. Several of his key executives had begun demanding that we teach their assistants all about STYLE in writing. They didn't like the writing "style" their aides employed in certain important communications written for their signature.

Here occurred the first (and only) time we found Bob at a loss for words about business writing and how he wanted it. When we questioned him as to what specifically the execs meant by style, he could only reply, "Damn if I know! I know what I like about a piece of writing in certain situations and what I don't like in others. Take some time off from your classes and try to find out what this style business is all about."

We were delighted to be able to shelve, even temporarily, classes on BLing and the battles over the mandatory BLing of suicidal information to irritable bosses. In compliance with Bob's orders, we agreed to conduct research on effective writing styles in business and shoved off into completely uncharted waters. Nobody, including us, had any idea whatsoever about what particular styles of writing worked best in which type of business situation — or even what these particular styles were!

We began by interviewing Bob's top people to see if they had anything to say that might enlighten us. But they had nothing to offer that was helpful. They not only expected their assistants to write accurate letters, memos and reports for their signatures; they also expected them to be able to make these documents sound as if each individual boss had actually written them. Style to them meant nothing more than "It has to sound like me!" This, of course, was ludicrous!

It was clear that no course on writing could be based on the idiosyncratic writing styles of all the bosses on the tenth floor of Bob's division! And it was also clear that no one style of writing could possibly be suitable for all message situations. Just as circumstances alter situations, circumstances alter how people express themselves when writing, say, to a friend or an enemy, or when writing to a superior or to an inferior, or when the message is good news or bad news.

Bob must have suspected that the executives who were raising hell about their assistants not writing the way they did were really complaining about something quite different, something these experienced, successful business people had trouble defining. They sensed that certain as yet undefined ways of writing seemed highly advisable in some message situations and absolutely disastrous in others. These top executives also knew, not just sensed, that what was wrong with many of the drafts of memos, letters, and reports written for their signature had nothing to do with BLing. It was some other aspect of writing that was bothering them.

Our BL course focused attention solely on the organization of information. It did NOT include a focus on whatever it was that was bugging these executives. We suspected that their complaints that drafts of letters written for their signature did not "sound like them" had more to do with the way something was expressed, than with how the letter was organized. "Style" was the word they had fallen back on. And every dictionary we consulted defined verbal "style" in terms of the "WAY" or "HOW" something is expressed.

HOW something is expressed often does make a difference in the effect it has on a reader. Here is the simplest of examples. You visit three different restaurants. On the door of the first restaurant is posted this sign: "No Shoes. No Shirt. No Service!" On the door of the second, "Shirt and Shoes Required" is posted. On the third, "Proper Attire is Expected."

Of course you see a difference in the effect each sign produces. Each is BLed admirably. But HOW that BL message is presented, and how it is received, is markedly different in each. What is subtly communicated gives potential customers a pretty good idea as to the probable clientele to be found in each place.

In the next chapter, we will give names to the styles of writing that are prevalent in business writing, and we will in future chapters give many illustrations of how certain styles work best in various sensitive message situations.

Defining Common Business Writing Styles

It's Not Only WHAT You Say, But HOW You Say It

Regardless of the reason that gave rise to the demand that we study business writing styles, the results were truly serendipitous. It turned out that a mastery of different writing styles proved to be something of extraordinary value to all who wanted to write successfully in various business situations, especially situations of a touchy nature. Of even greater importance to us selfishly was the fact that we learned how different styles of writing could be used to soften the impact of BLing and, hence, make the BLing of negative messages more acceptable to sensitive readers, like bosses!

THE VERY IMPORTANT OTHER 10%

There was no doubt that BLing is an absolute MUST in communications that merely exchange non-emotional information. And we had no basis on which to challenge Bob's estimate that 90% of all business communications were non-emotional exchanges. But BLing paid no attention to the realities of life involved in the other 10% of messages. Why? Because the types of messages found in this 10% contributed no more than a few drops to the "flood" of messages that were such a problem. Such is undoubtedly also true in today's e-mail world.

But these messages should not be ignored. For included in this 10% are some of the most difficult messages you may ever be called upon to write. How you handle them may exert a significant influence on how successful your career may be. Some of these 10% are painfully difficult, such as writing a letter firing a friend. Included also are message situations that are hazardous to write, such as one that refuses a favor to your biggest customer. But the most dangerous of all sensitive message situations to our trainees was that of telling the boss that his or her pet project, as currently developed, was a "turkey."

The greatest lode of gold our study of writing styles struck was that of learning how to make BLing more sensitive to readers' feelings and, hence, more persuasive. As the era of "control and command" began to end, the BLing of commands gradually became less effective. And the writing of persuasive messages that "got the job done" in situations where BLing alone might fail grew dramatically in importance. And there is no one to help you. Today, more than any time in history, business people are personally writing the vast majority of their own correspondence. Unless you are at the top of the heap, or very near to it, you write your own communications.

Therefore, what Bob forced us to learn about writing styles will be of considerable value to you. We ask you, please, to keep this firmly in mind for the next few pages which are, frankly, tedious. These pages will require you to read definitions and more definitions. Obviously, no one can discuss a complicated topic such as writing style without agreeing on some exact definitions of terms.

If you are interested only in controlling the flood of messages swamping the e-mail world, then skim the following pages. They are no fun to read. But don't throw the book away. Save it! You'd better, for the time surely will come when you are faced with a really tough writing situation, the success of which may make or break your career. At those times, believe us, you will rush back to these "boring" pages and find yourself devouring them with gusto.

Once you are familiar with our terminology, we promise to share many interesting illustrations of how this boring material can be used to enable you to write not only with economy, but with the sensitivity and persuasiveness required in delicate and sometimes dangerous situations. So, grit your teeth and stick with us. Here we go!

* * * * * * * * * * *

Our investigation began with defining the terms to be used in the study. This meant that we had to define and give labels to:

1. The generic types of messages commonly occurring in business.
2. The hierarchical directions in which messages are sent in the normal business day.
3. The various styles of writing common in business.

MESSAGE TYPES

You can imagine the number of different types of messages that daily flew around in Bob's division — purchase orders, requests for funding, approval or disapproval of certain proposed actions, approval or disapproval of requests for additional manpower, etc. You get the idea. We had to simplify this seemingly endless number of types of written communications into something basic, or generic. After much thought, we ended up deciding that some messages were simple exchanges of information that caused no reaction whatsoever. And then there were messages that caused strong emotional reactions in readers. Generically then, in terms of their effect upon a reader's EMOTIONS, there are two basic types of messages:

1. NONSENSITIVE MESSAGES. These constitute the vast majority of corporate communications. They are defined as mere exchanges of routine factual information which stimulate no emotional reaction in the reader. (Example: "If funding is available, I would like to add one new member to my team for these reasons...")

2. SENSITIVE MESSAGES. These messages do affect a reader's emotions, either positively or negatively:
   a. POSITIVE messages bring "good news." (Example: "Funds are available. You may hire the new team member.")
   b. NEGATIVE messages bring "bad news." (Example: "No funds are available for hiring a team member. Sorry.")
   c. PERSUASIVE MESSAGES must also be recognized as being sensitive. By their inherent nature, to be successful, persuasive messages can not merely convey routine,

factual information. What they convey has to exert a definite effect on a reader's emotions — either in a positive or in a negative way. Specifically:

—In POSITIVE-PERSUASIVE message situations, writers try to convince readers to take some action that readers can easily recognize as being for their own good. Thus, the message is emotionally pleasing and, hence, positive.

—In NEGATIVE-PERSUASIVE messages, the reverse is true. Here readers see nothing of self-interest in what the writer is "selling" and may even react to the request with strong distaste.

These distinctions about persuasive messages were unique, so far as we could determine. And it was a distinction that caused us many sleepless nights, trying to decide what organizational pattern and what style of writing was best in these persuasive message situations.

DIRECTIONS MESSAGES ARE SENT

In the environment of large business organizations at that time, there was, as our trainees forcefully pointed out, the very serious matter of the direction in which a message is sent. There are three possible directions:

1. UP is (a) when you are writing to a reader INSIDE your own organization who is more powerful, or of higher rank than you. UP is also (b) when you are writing to a reader OUTSIDE your organization who is, say, your biggest customer, or to an important state or federal governing agency. Bob, at first, scoffed at the notion that writing UP is in any way different from writing DOWN, but for once, we stuck to our guns.

2. DOWN is the opposite. You are in power over your reader, whether inside or outside of your organization. You are the boss — or you are the biggest customer. Writing DOWN is more fun and less hazardous that writing UP.

3. LATERALLY is when you are writing to someone (INSIDE or OUTSIDE of your organization) who is your equal in power — or where power is not an issue. These communications are usually routine and not

dangerous. (Frankly, in Bob's era, and even more so today, lateral writing is basically a free-for-all. No one seems unduly concerned about the organization or the style of messages sent laterally. BLing is of sole importance.)

THE FOUR MAIN STYLES

Today, the task of seriously studying and codifying the styles used in e-mail communications of various message types would be at most impracticable and at least impractical. However, in those days of hard-copy communications, we had easy access to thousands of copies of letters, memos and reports. And they were indeed written in differing styles depending upon a multitude of factors which we for the most part could not determine just by reading them. Did writer A write to reader B in a particular style because B did not like him or her? Or was B higher in authority than A? Often, not knowing the circumstances behind a message, we could not tell whether a message was one which would be regarded by the reader as positive or negative.

However, the actual identifying and labeling of the predominant types of writing styles we encountered was fairly easy for someone with a knowledge of high school grammar. Bob agreed that the styles of writing commonly used in his division could be classified into four distinct types: Forceful, Passive, Personal and Impersonal. Here is how we defined these four writing styles:

FORCEFUL STYLE

A Forceful style displays courage and imparts a sense of personal responsibility for what has been written. Used in the proper situation, it is highly effective. Used in the wrong situation, it can seem overbearing.

To write in a FORCEFUL STYLE:

  *Use the active voice. Make the subjects of sentences do things to people or objects, not just have things done to them.
  *Use the imperative — give orders! (Say "Correct this mistake immediately!" instead of "An immediate correction should be made.")

*Step up front and be counted. (Use the active voice. Say, "I have decided not to renew your contract," instead of using the passive voice: "After much deliberation and consideration of all factors involved, your contract will not be renewed.")
*Avoid using "weasel words" like "maybe," "possibly," "perhaps," or "it could be."

PASSIVE STYLE

In scientific and technical writing, the passive voice is the normal prose style employed. In business writing, the passive seems most useful in delicate message situations where the writer is consciously avoiding seeming overly forceful. It is also used when the writer feels it wise to disappear from the sentence — or at least not be at the forefront of the sentence.

To write in a PASSIVE STYLE:
*Use the passive voice as much as possible. (Write sentences in object-verb-subject order, not "I made a mistake," but rather "A mistake was made by me," or, even better, "A mistake was made.")
*Avoid the use of imperatives. (Say "Time is being wasted," instead of "Stop wasting time!")
*Avoid taking responsibility for negative statements by attributing them to faceless "others." (Say "It is possible that several objections to your plan might be raised by those hostile to its main objective," instead of "I have several objections to your plan." Or in an extremely delicate situation, you might even be forced to use "weasel words" if the going gets too rough.)

PERSONAL STYLE

A Personal style sounds like one human being talking directly with another. (This is essentially the style used in most of today's e-mail.)

To write in a PERSONAL STYLE:
*Use personal pronouns — especially "you" and "I."
*Use people's names (first names, if appropriate) instead of titles. (Say "Marge did a terrific job," instead of "Our team leader did a terrific job.")

*Use short sentences which capture the cadence of ordinary conversation. (Say "I discussed your idea with Paco. He's all for it!" instead of "Your proposal was discussed at Monday's meeting and was received favorably.")
*Ask questions of your reader. Say "How would you react to something like this? What are your thoughts?"
*Use contractions. Say "can't," "won't," etc. to sound conversational.

IMPERSONAL STYLE

An Impersonal style is, obviously, the converse of the Personal style. It is boring, pedantic, and finds its most apt use in message situations where the Forceful and the Personal styles seem inappropriate (or even dangerous).

To write in an IMPERSONAL STYLE:
*Avoid using people's names. If necessary, refer to them by title or job description.
*Avoid using personal pronouns, especially "I" and "you." ("We" may be all right to use when referring to one's organization.)
*Use long compound and complex sentences.
*Write long paragraphs.

(NOTE: There was one other style that showed up very infrequently, and then only in documents dealing with proposed advertising copy. That style, which we labeled "Colorful," made heavy use of adjectives, adverbs, fanciful similes and metaphors. This style was not included in the study. Bob vetoed the teaching of this colorful style, arguing that if anyone actually wrote to him, or to any of the executives he knew, in that style, he and they would fall out of their chairs laughing. Bob also was not overjoyed with any of the styles we had identified, except for Forceful and Personal. His view was simple: "Why doesn't everyone write like me?")

FINE TUNING THE RESEARCH

Once we had Bob's approval of all the terms to be used in the study, we felt we had to cut it down to size. We decided to review all message types and the directions in which they were sent. Then, based on our findings, we would decide which message situations were worthy of in-depth investigation, and which were not. Those where it did not matter what style of writing was used were immediately dropped from consideration.

It was obvious that style played no conceivable role in the success or failure of the 90% of messages that are nonsensitive. If a writer tells the reader what the current cost of a widget is, who cares about the style of writing that is employed? All a reader like Bob would care about was whether or not it was BLed, and that is a matter of how it is organized, not the style of writing used. Therefore, nonsensitive messages were deemed to be not worth studying and were given the axe.

A decision to drop simple "good news" messages from the study also was made. It seemed obvious that it would be foolish to research the effect of different styles on positive messages such as "You got the promotion, Betty. Congratulations!"

All that mattered about positive messages was that to be properly effective, they had to be BLed. Why would anyone not BL telling Betty something that would surely be music to her ears? And, if a writer did not BL a positive message like this one, it would badly damage the message's positive effect on Betty. We concocted the following non-BLed version of the letter to Betty to show to Bob as a justification of dropping positive messages from further consideration:

To: Betty
From: The Boss

As you would imagine, there were many excellent candidates for promotion in your area. This accounts for the delay in our arriving at a final conclusion as to the single candidate whose background and experience best prepare him or her for the responsibilities of the position.

After careful consideration, we have concluded that you will be promoted to that position beginning next week.

Bob thought this was pretty amusing, and quickly agreed that (a) the circuitous delaying of good news made the letter sound cold and begrudging, and that (b) if the writer had wanted to hurt Betty's feelings and take away some of her pleasure in hearing the news, this was a nasty, but subtle way to do it.

But he raised a very good question: "Doesn't the fact that you have not only changed the organization of the message, but also the style in which it is written, make it difficult to tell which of the changes — the writing style, or the new organization — has had the greater effect on Betty's emotions?" As usual, Bob was right. Both style and organization play important parts in messages which involve a reader's emotions, even positive ones like this.

We took special care, in all the case situations that we cooked up, to stick with one organizational pattern, and vary only the style used in the test memos developed for the study. Needless to say, that one organizational pattern was BL!

Creating cases would not present any significant problem, nor would the writing of stylistically different versions in response to the given case situation. What we needed was a sufficient number of people to react to our case situations so that their reactions would have some validity. It turned out, fortunately, that there was considerable interest in what we were doing, and many volunteered to serve. Some came from the ranks of the currently "shelved" trainee classes. Others came from those who had already completed the BL course. We were now ready to go.

Testing the Waters

One Size Fits All...Oh Yeah?

In order to learn about people's reactions to specific types of messages, we chose, temporarily, to study writing situations containing a single message. We deliberately ignored the fact that many business communications would contain more than one message. Later, when we had more experience in testing reader reactions, we would deal with communications containing a mixed bag of messages. One step at a time, for beginners.

Because BLing a negative message UP was such a touchy subject with many of the trainees who volunteered to serve on our panels, we decided to cater to their interests by beginning with two cases involving the writing of decidedly negative messages. We thought it prudent, however, to start with the easier, and less contentious case that involved sending a negative message DOWN, rather than UP.

For this case, as for all the cases we used in our study, we created different versions of memos written in response to the writing situation posed by the case. In this first case, each response was written in one of the four distinct pairs of style "opposites" being tested: Forceful versus Passive and Personal versus Impersonal. In order to ensure that readers' reactions were engendered by style differences alone, rather than by organization of thought, all sample memos were BLed. Here is that first case.

CASE I — NEGATIVE MESSAGE SENT DOWN

A Vice President has to write a memo to all headquarters department managers instructing them to set a good example for other employees by being more punctual about times of reporting to work and quitting. However, since this is a first reminder, and since some readers may, in fact, be blameless, the VP does not choose to issue a "Now hear this!" type of order. Pretend that you are the VP and you are considering which of the following BL draft versions of memos would be the best one to send to the department managers.

Memo I — FORCEFUL STYLE

All managers MUST set a good example for their subordinates. This means:
1. Report to work on time each day.
2. Do not quit work until 5:00 p.m. or later.

I must have your complete cooperation.

Memo II — PASSIVE STYLE

A good example will be set for subordinates if superiors report to work on time and depart not before 5:00 p.m. each day. Full cooperation will be expected.

Memo III — IMPERSONAL STYLE

The punctuality with which management reports to work in the morning and leaves in the evening sets an example for subordinates. Therefore, the announced beginning and ending times of work should be closely observed so as to make clear to all that punctuality is basic to a well-run organization.

Memo IV — PERSONAL STYLE

How do you think you would feel if your boss consistently reported to work later than you? Then made matters worse by leaving early? Not very good, I suspect.

Therefore, I know you will do all you can to set a good example for the people who report to you. In this tight economy, you and your fellow workers will want to make your full contribution to our company's efficiency and productivity.

PANELS' REACTIONS

*Memo I's Forceful style, they felt, exerts an extremely powerful emotional impact on its readers. This memo's style is perfect for the giving of orders. Each sentence is high impact because it is written in subject-verb-object order. The panels, however, overwhelmingly felt that the Forceful style used here made the writer sound like Captain Bligh on a bad day. This style, they believed, was entirely inappropriate in a first warning such as this, and that it fell into the "Now hear this!" tone the VP wanted to avoid.

*Memo II's Passive style seemed to them to produce a much, much weaker impact on the reader than that produced by the Forceful style of Memo I. However, the panels questioned whether this passive version, in its attempt to avoid sounding like Captain Bligh, went too far. Didn't it make the writer sound overly timid?

*Memo III's Impersonal style was, they felt, boring. It read like a textbook. They questioned how much this textbook style would weaken the memo's impact on readers? If so, is this reaction good or bad? Could a boring, impersonal style ever be desirable? And, if so, in what message situations would it fit? Clearly, this was a topic they recommended for further study.

*Memo IV's Personal style seemed to them to be "very chatty." It truly sounded like one person intimately conversing with another. But they all raised this question: "Is this chummy style appropriate in a really negative situation like this? By far, the panels voted overwhelmingly against the use of a Personal style in this situation. Most had difficulty expressing their reactions in words — they just felt it "jarred." In what situations might this style be more appropriate? This was another topic worth investigation.

Naturally, you, as a reader, would expect us to tell you which of the four styles used in these memos seems most appropriate in this situation. But we won't, for a very good reason. Just "telling" you answers will not work. This style business is very subtle. We, as well as our panels, learned only by collecting and analyzing our reactions to many, many case studies. You have to learn little by little, just as we did, what styles work in which message situations. The most instructive of these cases will be shared with you in the pages to come. When you have read and digested them, you will have learned what <u>we</u> gradually learned. You will then be able to make informed judgments about style choices facing you in difficult message situations like this one.

* * * * * * * * * * *

Our panels quickly became fascinated, as did we, with the style game we were playing. They had never thought, any more than we had, about distinct writing styles and which would work best in which situation. Next, we bit the bullet and gave them a case involving the most difficult single message situation of all. You know what case that would be.

Case II — NEGATIVE MESSAGE UP

You are a product manager who is obliged to respond to a request from the president of his corporation for written comments about a draft of a letter to stockholders. The final draft of the letter will be signed by the president and included in the company's annual report. The letter has been circulated to selected employees for their reactions. You discover some faults in the letter and must share these concerns frankly with the president in a BL fashion.

The panels had to decide which of the following memos to the president seemed most appropriate to this situation. The memos were labeled only as Versions I through IV. We did not reveal the style in which each was written.

Version I

To: Corporation President
From: Product Manager

Here are my comments about the proposed letter to stockholders you circulated for employee reaction:

1. *Don't come so close to a guarantee of increased profits in the fourth quarter. This is risky.*
2. *Stop being defensive about the company's performance this year. This insults those of us who worked as hard as we could.*

Version II

To: Corporation President
From: Product Manager

In reference to your request for employee comments about the proposed stockholder letter, the following observations could be made.

A guarantee of increased profits in the fourth quarter seems to be implied, and, as a result, a possibly unnecessary risk may be incurred.

Also, a less defensive posture could be taken about the company's performance this year. Such a posture would be appreciated by most employees.

Version III

To: Corporation President
From: Product Manager

I would like to give you my comments about your proposed letter to stockholders, which you circulated for our reaction:

1. If I were you, I don't think I would want to appear to be making a personal guarantee of increased profits in the fourth quarter. None of us would like to see you run the risk of building false expectations among stockholders.

49

2. I think you should also ask yourself this question: How do you think your own employees will react to this letter, not just how stockholders will react? If you do, I think you will come to the conclusion that this draft of the letter makes you sound very defensive about all of our performances this year. I know that I personally worked as hard as I could and I am sure that goes for the rest of the employees.

I hope these comments prove helpful to you as you set about deciding upon the final draft of the stockholder letter.

Version IV

To: Corporation President
From: Product Manager

Here are the requested comments about the proposed stockholder letter:

1. There is an implied guarantee of fourth-quarter profits that could inadvertently build unfounded stockholder expectations.

2. There appears to be a note of defensiveness about this year's corporate performance that could adversely affect employee morale.

PANELS' RESPONSES

We are sure you see, as clearly as our panels did, that Version I was written in a Forceful style. It is loaded with imperatives: "Don't do this" and "Stop doing that!" Every sentence is presented in a high impact subject-verb-object order. In fact, it is so forceful and brave that most panel members strongly felt it to be suicidal.

Version II uses a Passive style which allows the writer to fall back on a rhetorical trick prized among politicians. Its first sentence is written in the passive voice's object-verb-subject word order — except the writer has slyly omitted the subject, leaving it an unanswered question as to just WHO is making this objectionable "observation." The maker of the criticisms in the next two sentences also is absent. (Unfortunately, the letter had to be signed. But the writer gave it his or her best to disappear completely.) The panels voted strongly in favor of the passive version. Most of them thought it pretty clever in this situation.

Panelists were very much in conflict about the appropriateness of styles used in Versions III and IV. They liked the Personal style of writing, but on balance felt that this situation was not one where a warm, almost "chummy," style of expression was wise. They found the Impersonal Version IV cold and aloof, but much safer. Their votes ended up in a dead heat. Some combination of Passive and Impersonal seemed wisest.

So, this early in our testing, we had received some surprising reactions to various "single" message situations. In this case we were surprised to find out that two distinct styles, the Passive and the Impersonal, were simultaneously recommended, and strongly preferred over the Forceful or the Personal in a negative UP situation.

We learned that even in a communication containing only one message, a combination of two styles could be favored by sensitive readers. This revelation caused us to do some thinking, followed by a lot more testing. Here is a brief summary of what we found out about what is possible, and what is impossible, about style combinations:

1. In a single message, the Forceful and Passive styles cannot co-exist. Neither can the Personal and Impersonal styles. Both combinations are logically self-defeating.

2. The Passive and the Impersonal styles, however, are compatible and can be blended successfully in a single message.

3. The Forceful and the Impersonal styles can actually be blended, but only with great difficulty. The difficulty arises from the grammatical fact that the Forceful style relies heavily on the use of imperatives. But when one writes "Do this" or "Do that," it certainly is forceful, but it is also accidentally personal. In such imperatives, it is understood that <u>you</u> are to do this or that.

4. In multi-message letters, a writer can jump back and forth among any of our four styles, depending upon each message's probable effect upon the reader. Since most lengthy letters and reports contain several messages, the style (or style

combination) used for each message should depend on whether you want a given message to have a high or a low impact on the reader.

NO HELP ON BLing NEGATIVES UP

As we listened to the panels' discussions of styles in this first negative UP case, we got an earful of objections to the wisdom of BLing negatives UP. Not a single member of any of our panels felt that doing so was smart, or even polite. This reaction was identical to the ones we had been receiving, to our embarrassment and regret, in our classes.

Rather emphatically, the panels made it clear that they saw no reason why we should bother testing this universal rejection of BLing with additional negative UP cases. Past trainees who had volunteered to serve on the panels, and who had personally witnessed our fall from grace in the classroom over this topic, met with us privately. They urged us, for our own good, to do something about changing Bob's intransigence on the subject. Unfortunately, they had no suggestions as to how we could achieve this goal.

An Imaginary Meeting With Bob

"No!" Bob Explained

We were leery about rushing into a face-to-face meeting with Bob. So, instead, we played a mental game by imagining we were telling Bob exactly what we had learned in our style research and then speculating about what his probable responses would be. Here is a summary of what we, in our imagination, told him and an even briefer summary about what we felt he surely would tell us in response:

US: "In the 90 plus percent of messages that are nonsensitive, BLing works just fine. The style used does not matter and is not worth researching." BOB (Yawning): "O.K."

US: "In positive messages (especially those sent DOWN), a failure to BL the good news drastically reduces the positive impact on the reader, regardless of the style used." BOB (Looking pleased): "BLing is always good."

US: "In positive messages, UP or DOWN, a warm, Personal style is welcomed by readers. Despite the fact that many people worry about overusing the personal pronouns 'I' and 'we,' none of our panels found anything wrong with using either in positive messages." BOB (Shrugging): "Oh?"

US: "In negative messages, UP or DOWN, the Personal style seemed highly inappropriate in most instances." BOB (Waking up): "Why?"

US (Not answering the question, hurrying on): "In negative messages DOWN as well as UP, writers have to select the style that suits their purposes. If bosses want to sound tough, then they should choose the Forceful style. If they want to appear tough and be personal about it, they should choose a combination of the Forceful and the Personal styles." BOB: "Did you just answer my question about what's wrong with Personal? I don't think I heard it. I write personally and forcefully all the time. So what's so bad about that?"

US (Slyly): "If some superiors, not you, Bob, for reasons of their own, decide that they do not want to appear tough, or if they want to mute the impact of a particularly negative message, they should select the Passive style. Both the Passive and the Impersonal styles give the writer a chance to hide out, instead of marching at the head of every active voice sentence. If they want, for some reason, to distance themselves even more from their negative message, then they should use a combination of the Impersonal and the Passive styles." BOB: "This is ridiculous! I always use a Forceful style. I'm always Personal. And I BL everything. I've never had any trouble whatsoever! What is the matter with young people today?"

* * * * * * * * * * * *

Our imaginary visit with Bob was clearly a disaster. Any progress report we could make would have to admit that our findings rejected, in the strongest of terms, his insistence on BLing negative messages UP. But that would be a waste of time. He would just listen with half an ear. He wouldn't want to hear our troubles. He was really only interested in hearing about the success we had in learning how to make the BLing of negative messages UP palatable through the deft use of some yet to be discovered sleight of stylistic pen.

THE BULL GETS THROWN

The members of our panels were far from stupid. They knew, without us telling them (which we had not), that the pressure on us to demand the BLing of negative messages UP came from Bob. And they knew we were stalling around, reluctant to report to Bob that, as yet, we had discovered no stylistic way to make BLing UP palatable. So they took matters into their own hands.

They had, without our knowledge, cooked up a case situation that could possibly bring the issue with Bob to a head. They had invented a case about a tough boss, who they named "Bull," and essentially commandeered some of our scheduled research time to experiment with varying ways to tell Bull something he did not want to hear. We got tipped off as to what they were up to, and invited ourselves in to observe the festivities.

They had divided themselves into small groups and assigned to each the job of writing a BLed memo to Bull telling him that something he wrote stank! They voted on which group had created the most insulting memo. This is the memo that was chosen:

To: Bull
From: Your Administrative Assistant

Pages one to ten of your draft report on possible new marketing opportunities are boring. Unfortunately they are the most entertaining of the entire twenty pages.

Cries of "Don't I wish" and the like rang out. One wit shouted: "Dear Bull. Your last ten pages are terrific, compared to the first ten." More laughter. The group leader told them to get serious and to create a revised memo that would do the job without loss of scalp or tail. The groups had a go at it. Here was the "winning" version:

To: Bull
From: Your Administrative Assistant

It is possible that some readers of the proposed report might possibly find it even more persuasive if the last ten highly interesting pages were presented first, and were supported by selected paragraphs drawn from the first ten pages.

The group was actually surprised by this effort. The writers had cleverly used a combination of Impersonal and Passive styles which allowed the fictional writer to be as invisible as possible. They had wisely put the burden of finding fault with Bull's report on to the heads of "some readers" who were unknown. It was widely agreed that the writers of this effort had a great future in politics!

Next, the leader asked the breakout groups to write a memo in response to a situation where there were no convenient nine pages of good stuff in Bull's draft report to put positive emphasis on. Now Bull's draft report was no good from beginning to end. They tried valiantly, but nothing worked. No silk purses out of sow's ears resulted. One young man, who had been scribbling away quietly in a corner seat, stood up and said, "Take a look at this approach. Could I get away with it? Or not?" He put his draft on the screen.

To: Bull
From: Your Administrative Assistant

Since I do not have the necessary depth of knowledge about the subject covered in your proposed report on new marketing opportunities, I found it impossible to judge the reaction of others whose marketing knowledge and experience so far exceed mine. I have read the report over several times. Each reading confirmed my feelings of inadequacy. I am very sorry that I was not, and am not, able to be of assistance to you.

This version stimulated considerable discussion. Comments varied greatly. Some thought it a very clever and well written dodging of responsibility. Others thought it was unrealistic. Why would an employee who was completely ignorant about marketing be assigned as an administrative assistant to a marketing manager? They felt that the memo just wouldn't "fly." Others felt that if it didn't fly, the writer could be in "serious trouble — dereliction of duty, or something like that."

But this comic romp with Bull had served its purpose. It taught us that the use of the Passive and the Impersonal styles did, indeed, do much to soften the impact of a BLed negative message. But we knew that Bob detested the Passive style's attempts to shield, or outright hide, the writer from responsibility for what he or she wrote. He would reject the Impersonal style too, we felt, for the same reason. Bob hated dishonesty of all types, and he would feel that stylistic dodging around was dishonest.

We had to make Bob face the fact that people like him who could take hard truths stylistically unsoftened, and BLed to boot, were hard to find in positions of authority in any organizational hierarchy — business, military, religious, or political!

Our Counterattack

Life Jackets Come in Plus Sizes

We were caught in the middle. Bob continued to approve our consulting fees without complaint, but the trainees had the potential to continue humiliating us with bad ratings. And, in truth, there was more than money and bad ratings on our mind. We also deeply wanted to regain the respect of our trainees. The majority of them, once they understood our situation, had been more than patient with us. We simply had to figure out some way to convince Bob that, for once in his life, he actually could be WRONG! And to have even the slightest hope of accomplishing that, we had to devise some way to make Bob discover for himself WHY he was wrong.

We invented a case tailor-made to put him on the spot. It was designed to force him to practice what he preached to others. We led him to believe we had an especially difficult case intended for use in the new style program and wanted his help with it. The case put Bob in the role of a corporate VP — this he could easily identify with. But we made this VP face writing an extremely negative message, ostensibly DOWN, but actually, UP. We told him we were absolutely stumped. Here is that case.

NEGATIVE MESSAGE UP and DOWN CASE

You are the newly appointed, and very recently hired, VP for Production of a medium-size corporation. You decide to write to the purchasing managers in each of your production facilities and tell them that from now on, they must request your approval of any contracts in excess of $50,000. You realize that this is clearly a negative message, since having to go back and forth with you while they're trying to get the best price from the supplier will be time wasted in their mind. Second, they will feel injured professionally, since this sharp reduction in their discretionary power can hardly be viewed as a vote of confidence by the new VP. And you also realize that offending these very competent executives is not a good way to begin your relationship with them. So, in a very real way, this message is being written both UP and DOWN. Yet you strongly feel that this step must be taken. How should this communication be organized and in which style or styles should it be written?

Bob finished reading and looked up. "What do you want me to do? Play the role of the VP?"

We told him. "Yes, but not yet. Later. We really need your advice about how you think we should teach the case. So, just imagine it's you, not one of us, standing in front of a class of trainees. Suppose a young trainee raises her hand and says to you, 'We know you'd want this memo BLed. You want everything BLed! So what style of writing do YOU think would help make BLing such a terribly negative message as this ever be successful?' Well, Bob, she's asked a fair question. What's your answer?"

Bob shrugged. "How do I know? Can the effect of a BLed negative message UP actually be softened by the right style choice? You're the guys doing the study. You tell me." He pointed to the white board on his office wall. "Show me how a BL first sentence of this letter would look if written in the different styles."

We went to the board and wrote:

FORCEFUL STYLE: All purchasing managers MUST receive prior approval from me for any contracts being negotiated that will be in excess of $50,000.

"O.K.," Bob said. "Now let me see it in the Passive."

PASSIVE STYLE: A decision has been made that all contracts in excess of $50,000 must be approved by headquarters prior to negotiation.

Bob laughed. "That Passive version is awful! It makes me look as if I'm hiding under a rock, pretending I'm not the one who made this decision. Wouldn't work! Purchasing would know instantly that a power grab like this had to be approved by me. My stock with them would go down like the Titanic!"

"Well, what about the Forceful version?"

"I think it's fine in a situation where I'm trying to let someone know who's boss. But the way the case states it, I'm trying to finesse this situation. Get the idea across without foolishly ticking off what are apparently valued execs. So I don't think I'd be smart being that forceful in this instance. But," he said, holding his nose, "I sure didn't like that turkey of a Passive version. Let me see if the other styles have anything to offer."

PERSONAL STYLE: I have decided that all contracts in excess of $50,000 being negotiated by you and all other purchasing managers must have prior approval by me.

IMPERSONAL STYLE: Contracts in excess of $50,000 are to be approved by my office prior to negotiation.

Bob showed interest. "Although I didn't know it before, I've always normally written in the Personal style. That Impersonal version is just as BLed as the Personal is, but I've got to admit it, the Impersonal sounds better, somehow. Doesn't sound so much big ME, little YOU, as the Personal version did."

We thought we had scored a point. Bob was actually questioning the appropriateness of one of his pet styles of writing — at least in a case

61

like this. So to tightly wrap up this concession, we bluntly asked him to specify which of these two styles he would choose in this situation.

Bob sat quiet for a short while, deciding on his answer. When he finally gave it, we were absolutely astounded. "Neither!" he said. "Look, this case is more than all right in helping someone like me realize the way each style affects a reader differently. And, just so you don't think I'm stupid, I want to tell you that I know you're trying to make a point with me about the hopelessness of BLing something negative UP. But this case won't do the job, because it's not realistic. It attempts to force me to WRITE something, regardless of whether or not it's smart to put a difficult message like this in writing."

Our mouths hung open.

Bob continued, "Personally, I would never trust success to a single written communication in a highly negative situation like this — that is, UNLESS I knew what I wrote would be accepted by my readers, not as an insult, or an attempt to clip their wings, but as an idea worth consideration."

Bob stopped. He seemed just as surprised as we were by what he had just told us. He looked at his watch and drew a deep breath. "Time to go. Very interesting case. But you'd better do some thinking about it. Not realistic. See you later." Then he was gone.

We didn't see him again for about a week. We stayed busy working up style materials. Then one morning, Bob stuck his head in our office door. "I still say you guys got it all wrong! What you ought to be focusing on is NOT the creation of situations where it is strategically stupid to write anything at all! You're supposed to be teaching writing, for God's sake! Not NOT writing!" And off he went.

We grinned at each other. "At least we've got him thinking." Later that day, Bob looked in on us again, shook his head disgustedly, and disappeared. More days passed without event. We stayed busy but anxious. Finally, Bob's secretary called, telling us that Bob wanted to see us in his office at four o'clock. We got even more nervous.

The moment we got in his office, Bob started talking. "I'm bothered by something. You remember my telling you the other day that I wouldn't put in writing such a highly negative message as that damn case poses?" We told him we remembered. "And I qualified that statement by saying something like 'unless I knew that what I wrote would not be considered as an insult by my reader.' You noticed?" We told him that we had noticed.

"Well, that's been bothering the hell out of me." We looked concerned. "Is it possible," Bob said in a muffled voice, "that I was feeling much the same as the trainees do when they balk at BLing negative ideas in writing to their bosses?" We agreed that was possible.

Bob left his chair and stood looking out of his window. "You know," he said, "I remember very well the time you guys told me that the reason I couldn't understand the trainees' problem was because 99% of what I wrote was sent DOWN. And that 100% of what the trainees wrote was going UP to their boss or indirectly to their boss's boss."

He turned and pointed his finger at us. "You cooked up that damn purchasing managers case, didn't you? Just for me." We didn't say a word. "You were trying to force me to write from an insecure position, not as insecure as the trainees' position, of course. But you got me playing the role of a newly appointed VP writing to some very valuable and experienced executives that I couldn't afford to tick off. And for the first time in an awfully long time, I was having to face writing a very tough negative message UP.

"So then I surprised myself by immediately rejecting the Forceful style version, even though that's the way I customarily write. And I ended up choosing an Impersonal style, which also is not how I usually write. Your case had me on the run. But I didn't retreat all the way back to choosing the Passive version, thank God! But I was still retreating. And why? That's what intrigues me." He sat back again, resignedly, into his chair. "So, there you are. Given the right situation, I'm just as chicken as the trainees! I didn't like BLing something this negative UP any more than they do!"

He told us that this recognition was very disturbing to him because he now felt caught between the proverbial rock and a hard place. He repeated his old fear that if he gave most of the trainees the slightest justification to ignore BLing when writing a negative message UP, they would revert to their old ways. "The moment I take my foot off their necks, they'll start wasting everybody's time with long, diffuse memos, regardless of the situation.

"Corporations run on information," he said. "And timely information that is bad news is often just as important, if not more important, than good news. Hell's bells! Good news, you don't have to do anything about, except cheer. But bad news, you damn well better do something about — and quick! And if bad news is blocked from being passed UP, something is drastically wrong."

"Wait just a minute, Bob," we interrupted. "The trainees haven't complained about having trouble BLing some bad news to their boss about something like, say, a competitor undercutting their company's prices. What they complain about is having to BL a memo to their boss that he or she's written a lousy report or something personally insulting like that. The message about price-cutting is a factual statement of bad news; no reason in the world not to BL it. Telling the boss his report is lousy is also bad news, but it's far different; it's bad news that is personally offensive."

Bob glared at us. "How in the world did this damn confusion ever get started?"

We had no hesitation; we had spent days thinking about our answer. "Our best guess is it started way back when the BL training program was just beginning. We opened with an exercise which forced students to identify the BL in memos we got from your secretary. Then we made them apply the 'So What?' test you taught us to the various messages that were included in your reports and memos. Naturally, the message that passed your 'So What?' test always turned out to be the most important message in each document. And your instructions to us were that, since it was the most important message, it <u>must</u> be BLed. There were to be no exceptions. You remember telling us that?" Bob nodded.

"And in almost all memos, that's exactly where it does belong — so long as the message that passed the 'So What?' test is not highly offensive to the reader. That important qualification, we never mentioned. And why wasn't it? Because, in those original memos your secretary sent us, people had written them to you. So, they were all written UP. Not surprisingly, there was not a single letter in that heap that had even the slightest chance of being offensive to you. Certainly, nothing of the 'your report stinks' variety, needless to say.

"All we were preparing to teach, all we were concerned with, was drawn from real-life examples of clear, no nonsense, BLed communication. And that's what we taught from. We never thought about sensitive messages. We judged the business world by the samples of memos and letters you received. They were all factual; they were never emotional. The only emotion we ever saw was when you would get sore because something was not BLed. We really got blindsided when the lousy evaluations poured in."

"I'm sorry," Bob said. "I've seen those poor performance evaluations you were getting. I think those trainees…"

We cut him off. "No, Bob. Don't blame them. They were only giving back to us exactly what we had taught them — say what you mean without beating around the bush."

"So," Bob asked, "where do we go from here? We are all in a hole, apparently caused by a series of accidents. As for me, I don't want to take my foot off their necks about BLing, you know that. But I'll be damned if I want you to continue taking this kind of beating for doing what I've told you to do."

"Listen, Bob," we said. "If you will agree, just between us, to one little change, we can continue teaching BLing as the main focus of effective business writing."

"What kind of change?"

"It's a change that will be automatically built-in when we add style to the BL program. No fanfare. No mention of anything out of the ordinary. We keep hammering, as usual, on the point that BLing saves time for them and money for the corporation. We breeze into making the point that most written communications contain more than just one message. In passing, we suggest that in the extremely rare situation where the most important message, the one that passes the 'So What?' test, is guaranteed to offend or incense the reader, they should look for some other message to BL. This is the ONLY time they should ever consider NOT BLing the most important message. And we point out to them over and over that such message situations are an extremely rare exception to the rule, and certainly NOT an invitation to stop BLing everything else."

Bob was very interested. "But," he said, "won't some trainees still be scared? Even if the negative message to their boss is not BLed, it will still be there."

"Some may be worried. But that's life. It's true, some of their bosses may actually be so insecure or vain that they can't stand constructive criticism. But, fortunately, that's where style really can help. There are delicate ways of telling someone something he or she doesn't want to hear."

"You're referring to the Passive style. And the Impersonal. The ones I don't like."

"You've got it. Look, one administrative assistant writes this to his boss, 'I think the evidence you cite in your proposed report is quite weak in points one, two and three.' Another smarter assistant might write, 'It could be that some persons, unsympathetic to your ideas, might conclude that the evidence you have marshaled in support of your argument needs a bit more development.'"

"Wouldn't fool me," Bob snorted.

"It probably wouldn't fool that boss either, but the way it is expressed seems more polite, less superior, less *smart me* and *stupid you*."

"O.K., it's a deal," Bob said, standing and glancing at his watch. "So let's summarize exactly what we have agreed to. You will tell your classes, as soon as they can be resumed, that the primary emphasis of the writing course remains on BLing, for that's where the greatest savings of time and money are to be found. But the writing jobs they perform will also require that they determine, in highly sensitive, usually strongly negative message situations, what is the SMARTEST message to BL!

They have to figure out in these rare, but often very critical situations, what is the most reader-sensitive organization of ideas possible."

We were extremely pleased. We quickly agreed. To celebrate, Bob suggested we call it a day and go have a drink. Over our second round, we told Bob with great glee about the panels' attempts to BL "your proposed draft stinks" to the irascible "Bull." "Know what?" Bob said, "Go back to those kids working with you on the panels and tell them I said this: 'If I had a boss who was that conceited and vindictive, I'd read his report and tell him it was wonderful!' To hell with trying to help him. Let the son of a bitch sink."

Just before we adjourned our celebration, Bob asked whether we had covered everything dealing with style. We told him no, that we hadn't even touched persuasive messages. "When you get through with persuasion, what kind of course are you going to end up with? What in the world can we call it? I don't like getting the term 'style' into it. Sounds like something out of the fashion industry to me. Besides, the deal we've made calls for the focus to remain on BLing."

"But with sensitivity added to it," we reminded.

"So why don't we just call the new course BLPLUS? BLing plus sensitivity!"

We told him he couldn't have chosen a better name, and heaved simultaneous sighs of relief.

Bob
on
Persuasion

Making Silk Purses...

It was a good thing that Bob had agreed to help us with persuasive messages. We were babes in the woods about the supposed "art" of persuasion and particularly about how to apply it to negative-persuasive messages. Admittedly, a negative-persuasive DOWN message shouldn't be nearly as much of a problem, we thought, simply because it should be a lot easier for writers who are "one up" on their readers to "persuade" them to do something they otherwise might not choose to do. But for the subordinate to persuade a superior or a big customer to take an action the reader saw nothing of self-interest in doing was a horse of quite another color.

Persuasion, positive or negative, was (and is) a complex topic. One problem is that all communications, to a degree, must be persuasive — if only by the necessity of persuading a recipient to read the message in the first place. Of course we knew that BLing a communication played an important part in persuading a busy recipient to read it. Bob's instinctive reaction to a non-BLed report was to send it back to the writer, unread, accompanied by a two-word commentary: "BL it!"

So to hard-nosed executives like Bob, BLing was a premier persuasive inducement to read any given message, including negative-persuasive messages sent UP to them. But to other, less hardy readers, the BLing of a highly negative message to them was clearly super nonpersuasive.

Instead of persuading them to read further, a BLed first paragraph that hit them with a request to do, buy, or believe something they had no use for, seemed sure to fail. And that's the definition we had given to a negative-persuasive message.

At our meeting with Bob, we told him that while we had no trouble BLing positive-persuasive messages, we had big trouble doing the same with negative-persuasive ones. "You know," we said, "persuading someone to get a flu shot or to sign up for a vacation is child's play. You simply BL it. But persuading someone to take a pay cut, or give up his or her vacation is quite a different kettle of fish."

This statement vastly amused Bob; he immediately burst out laughing. "You guys occasionally surprise me. Sometimes you seem smart but sometimes you seem pretty damn dumb. This is one of the dumb times." He laughed some more; then he apologized. "Know why I'm laughing? It's because you haven't stumbled onto the simple fact that there's no difference between the way negative- or positive-persuasive messages should be handled."

"Are you kidding?" we asked, quite seriously. "There's a world of difference. Just by definition. The reader asks, 'What's in it for me?' If the answer is 'nothing,' the message is negative-persuasive. If the answer is 'something,' then it is positive-persuasive."

"Oh," Bob said airily, "I admit there is that difference, but so what? Pay no attention to it. You're just playing with words. To be successful, you have to approach a negative-persuasive situation exactly as you would a positive-persuasive one."

We demanded to know what in the world he was talking about. "Look," he said, pointing his finger at us, "I peddled technical products and services for years, and I tell you, there's no difference in the way the two types of persuasive messages should be handled — that is, if you know how to sell. Which you guys obviously don't!" He snickered again. He was having fun. "All successful salesmen know they have to focus solely on the benefits potential customers will get as a result of buying the product. That makes it a positive-persuasive message in my book."

"But it's still negative-persuasive in the customer's mind."

"So what?" said Bob, laughing again. "If customers weren't negative, if they were already sold on the product, I wouldn't have had a job. I wouldn't have been needed. Customers would have been rushing to get their orders in before their competition did."

"So you're telling us that it doesn't matter if the potential customer is antagonistic to the very notion of what you are selling. It only matters if those doing the selling are completely convinced that their product is the cat's pajamas?"

"Damn right! Personally, I'd have to be absolutely convinced that my product was great or I wouldn't be selling it in the first place. And I would have shown my confidence in my product by BLing my sales pitch, not burying it as if I were ashamed of it. I'd tell them right off the bat, 'I want to sell you the best damn product in the world. Let me show you how it will help you and improve the profitability of your company.' And I'd tell them. No bull. No beating around the bush. It's the same whether you're talking or putting it in writing."

"If that's the case," we asked, "why in the world do so many people think it smart, even necessary, to be extremely circuitous in presenting their sales pitches? Every week we get letters trying to sell us things like one more credit card and every letter is at least two pages long, some longer. If these letters didn't work, wouldn't they do something different?"

Bob rolled his eyes. "I'd bet any amount of money that you don't really read any of that crap you get. You toss them in the trash as fast as I do. Besides, there is absolutely no correlation between what works in direct mail and what is persuasive in all other business operations. Direct mail is hit and run; it's faceless entities writing to faceless readers who are no more than names on a list."

Bob continued, "In a company like this one, we are writing mostly to people we regularly work with or do business with, people we know, at least professionally. The kind of persuasive communication people in businesses like mine need to master is not hit and run. So you guys stop wasting your time worrying about whether long-winded, circuitous approaches are the way to handle negative-persuasive messages. Just think positive and BL them!"

POSITIVE THINKING

The key to being persuasive, according to Bob, was to become an absolute optimist. You must be able and willing to try to find something positive to emphasize, even in the gloomiest of situations. The old song, "accentuate the positive," was what Bob wanted us to sing. We asked if he had a simple example of being positive that we could use in future classes. He promised he would look for one.

A few days later, Bob phoned and asked us to stop in. He said he had a really good, short and sweet case for us to consider. When we met, he told us that, some time ago, we had asked him to find us an example of a piece of writing in which there were different messages "hidden in plain sight." He said he never could find one; so he made one up. It had been sitting on his desk ever since. He said he felt it would work equally well as an example of positive thinking in a pretty tricky negative-persuasive UP situation. He handed us this letter:

Dear Biggest Customer:

We are terribly sorry for the delay in the delivery of your order of Feb. 17th which we accidentally shipped to Comstock, MN, instead of Comstock, MI.

After reading it, we just stared at him. We didn't get it.

"How many times do I have to tell you guys to think positively? I suppose all you are thinking about is how hard it will be to persuade this guy not to be sore at you for screwing up? That's just a waste of time. Learn to think positive! Imagine you're the big customer. Look at the first words of the letter, at what is BLed! 'We are terribly sorry…' Are these really positive words? No! Is the customer interested in hearing how sorry you are for the foul up? No! But, is there something, even remotely positive, that he might want to hear? How about this?" He handed us another version.

Dear Biggest Customer:

Your Feb. 17th order will arrive at your plant in Comstock, MI, on March 2nd by air freight from Comstock, MN, where it was erroneously sent, owing to a shipping error.

Bob pointed out that not only was this single sentence BLed, it also BLed the most positive opening sentence possible under the circumstances. "It doesn't waste time boohooing and crying Mea Culpa, which the customer probably doesn't care a rat's derrière about. He wants to know when he's going to get his shipment! Now, that's thinking positively and BLing it to boot!"

"But where is the persuasive part?" we asked.

"Isn't it obvious? The persuasion lies in my taking prompt action to meet <u>his</u> needs. It also lies in my refusal to cater to <u>my</u> need always to be in the right. I could have tried to put the blame on the Post Office. Argued that it's their fault for using MI for Michigan and MN for Minnesota when both states start with the letters MI. Most people would do just that. And why? To justify themselves, and to hell with focusing on the reader's need for a quick correction of the mistake. People don't like to hear other people's justifications of their mistakes. That's just being self-serving, and being self-serving is not being persuasive, believe me!"

"What about offering an apology?"

Bob shrugged. "If the writer thinks it wise and proper to apologize, then doing so briefly in the last sentence might be appropriate."

We walked away from this meeting wondering out loud — that if what Bob had told us about persuasion was correct and that simple, what need was there for us to develop cases to test how negative-persuasive messages should be handled? Bob had stated most forcefully that they should be handled in exactly the same way. Select the most positive message possible, BL it, and use some appropriate combination of the Forceful and the Personal styles.

We discussed Bob's position with a few of the leaders of our panels. They thought that Bob was right in both respects — that beating around the bush when trying to sell something doesn't work. "BLing is better," they said, "Shows confidence." And they personally thought that it was probably a waste of time to cook up cases and check panel reactions to negative- and positive-persuasion cases, UP or DOWN. They unanimously agreed with Bob that a blend of the Forceful and Personal styles would be what panels would choose.

NEGATIVE PERSUASIVE UP MESSAGES

We conferred next with Bob, told him that we were through with testing, and that BLPLUS was just about ready to go. We explained that we were going to rely on him to give us some good, real-life cases involving negative-persuasive messages sent UP. His reply was "Sure. When do you want them?" We told him as soon as possible. Within a day or two, Bob gave us the following example with the letterhead of Community General Hospital.

Dear Bob,

As you know, I respect your professional opinion highly. The advice your people have given us at ABCA Corporation over the past three years has been most helpful.

I am writing to you now, however, in my new role as Chairman of the Executive Committee of our hospital's Board of Trustees. We have decided to establish a team of skilled volunteers to help us assess proposals to further improve our hospital's information flow.

I have suggested your name to my committee as a member of that evaluation team. I know you would get real satisfaction from helping your community in this way. Please say yes. I look forward to being able to count on your advice. Let me hear from you soon.

Cordially,

Samuel J. Spears

After we read it, we asked Bob for the background facts. He told us that Spears was the VP of Finance for ABCA Corporation, a very good customer of Bob's company. Bob said he knew Spears pretty well, having worked with him on several community service projects. We asked him what was so tough about this letter. "Well," he responded, "if I say no, I'll be displeasing a valued customer. But if I say yes, I'll find myself in a conflict of interest situation for as long as I am on the Board — and possibly for some time after."

"How so?"

"Because my company is always submitting proposals for upgrading the information flow in every complicated field — including hospital administration. And Community Hospital would be off limits for us to solicit business if I ended up on their evaluation team, judging proposals. Even if I recused myself from voting on my company's proposals, it still could be argued that I had bad-mouthed proposals from other companies. And even after I was off the team, I'm sure someone could easily find a lawyer happy to make a claim that my company's getting some future contract or other was actually a payoff for my earlier services."

"What are you going to do?"

"I'll have to tell him no, but I need to do it with kid gloves. He's accustomed to getting his own way on everything."

"Well," we said. "Very interesting. A perfect case of the irresistible force meeting the immovable object."

Bob was not amused, "Let's get down to business," he said, gruffly. "First, what type of message are we dealing with here? Obviously, what you guys call negative-persuasive. He's trying to 'persuade' me to do what I do NOT see as being in my own and my company's best interests. And since he is the big customer, he is writing DOWN and I'm responding UP. Let's dissect his letter and see what we can learn." Bob began the dissection. "Spears wisely begins on a positive note, by praising me," Bob said. "But then he immediately bootlegs in a reminder that for the last three years, his company, ABCA, has been a big customer of ours."

We took over, "In paragraph two, when he tells you that he's just become the Chairman of the Executive Committee, he's announcing that he's now part of the inner circle of movers and shakers at the hospital. That puts more pressure on you to accept. He subtly warns you that telling him 'no' may lead to the loss of future business not only with ABCA, but also with the hospital.

"Paragraph three: Now that he's let you know he's got you in two ways, he figures out yet another way to put pressure on you. He tells you that he, personally, has suggested your name to his board. Meaning, don't make me look like a fool! Don't let me down in front of my new committee! Please say yes!"

"Wow! This guy is something," we said to Bob. "Notice how cleverly he uses the Personal style. Three times he uses the little word 'I' in the last paragraph alone. It makes it seem all the more a personal affront if you don't do as he asks."

"Well, he's done a damn good job of writing a hard-nosed negative-persuasive letter DOWN, I've got to admit it," Bob said. "Be tough to answer." We did not disagree. Bob hesitated. We took the hint. "Give us an hour or so to work on an equally slick negative UP message for you to consider sending. If we're lucky," we said, "we'll cook up, not just one, but several possibilities to consider when we come back."

That afternoon, we met Bob at his office and gave him the following three drafts of possible responses to Spears. We deliberately did not label the style used in the three different versions because we knew that Bob would immediately veto any version labeled either Passive or Impersonal. And we strongly felt that either the Passive, the Impersonal, or a combination of the two would be the safest choice.

VERSION I

Dear Sam,

As you realize, this litigious age makes it necessary for large companies often to take stringent measures not only to avoid conflicts of interest on the part of their employees, but also to preclude even the very suggestion of conflict. And, since my company intends to submit a proposal with reference to improving the hospital's information flow, it would not appear seemly for me to be part of an evaluation team assessing proposals from competitors. Even if I were to recuse myself from consideration of any proposal presented by my corporation, I still would be vulnerable to charges that I gave short shrift to competitors' offerings.

If there is any other way that I can serve the committee that will not raise this conflict of interest specter, you know that I would find it pleasurable to be of service as always.

VERSION II

Dear Sam,

Your comments relative to your respect for my professional opinion are most appreciated. Moreover, your invitation to serve on the hospital's contract evaluation team is received with gratitude, albeit with some concern.

The evaluation team must be composed of persons who are free of alliances with any of the vendors submitting proposals. For that reason, it is felt that my services on the team could be construed as a conflict of interest.

Perhaps help can be given in some other way. Again, please be assured that your invitation has been greatly appreciated.

VERSION III

Dear Sam,

Thanks for suggesting my name as a possible member of your contract evaluation team. I really wish I could serve, but I cannot.

Naturally, my company intends to submit a proposal for upgrading the hospital's information flow. You can see the position of conflict I would be in if I were on the evaluation team.

Just let me know of any other way I can be of help. You know I will be more than willing. Thanks again for the invitation.

Bob read each version through carefully, then read them once more, pausing to think for a moment after each. Then he told us, "I'll pick Version III."

We asked how he arrived at his decision. "Well," he said, "it's obvious that the task at hand is to create a negative-persuasive message written UP that can effectively trump a tough negative-persuasive message written DOWN. But trumping means succeeding in telling him 'no' in such a way that it doesn't seem offensive.

"Version I seems cold, impersonal and complex to me. It seems brainy, but aloof. I think its big words alone would turn Spears off. It certainly lacks persuasiveness. Spears doesn't give a damn about any potential legal troubles of mine; yet, that's what the entire letter focuses on. Furthermore, it never has the guts actually to tell him 'no.' It merely tells him all the reasons that would add up to a 'no' answer. I don't like it. Neither would Spears."

We told him that we believed many people would write a very similar, legalistic, "textbook" letter like Version I in a situation like this. Bob responded that he didn't care what many people would do. We asked him how he liked Version II.

"Version II," Bob told us, "also seems cold." Then Bob surprised us by showing that he had been boning up on our style terminology. "Its style is quite Impersonal, but it is also written in the Passive." He cited: "'Your comments…are most appreciated'; 'Your invitation…is received'; 'it is felt that…'; 'your invitation has been greatly appreciated…' I know you guys might argue that some combination of the Passive and the Impersonal styles might well be the best choice to send a tough old bird like Spears, but, damn it, it's just not me, and Spears would know it was phony. And sounding phony is NOT what being persuasive is all about!"

We asked what he thought of Version III. "Now this version is right up my alley. You knew, of course, that I would want to BL this message if I could possibly get away with it. I wasn't sure that I could. But you did it.

Damn, but I admire that first paragraph! It's BLed, but you've made everything seem positive. You've got me first saying 'Thanks.' Then 'I wish I could, but I can't.' That really works. Then you don't hand him all that stuff about lawyers and potential legal troubles. What does he care about all that crap? That's my problem, not his. What he has to care about, if anything is going to work in this case, is that I have given him my word in writing that I will be 'more than willing' to help on something that is possible for me to do. You've got me saying 'no' in a positive way and giving him something in return, my promise to help the next time. Good job! I'll send Version III out first thing tomorrow morning."

...FROM A SOW'S EAR

On another day Bob breezed in waving a letter. "Here's a beauty! I just love this guy's letter. Had to show it to you." It was from a Mr. A. J. Henry, who was the manager of a large private golf club close to the city. It was addressed to Bob and read:

I just received your company's list of increased maintenance charges. I am at a loss to understand the justification for two price increases in one two-month period.

[Mr. Henry then included a paragraph complaining that maintenance charges on Product A had increased 16% and Product B, 12%.]

If we raised the price of golf like you do, soon everyone would be playing ping-pong instead! It would be nice if we could just pass price increases along the way you do, but our members wouldn't like it any more than I do. Could you explain?

"Before I ask you how you would handle a response to this letter," Bob said, "let me brief you on the facts about this situation. First, Henry is wrong. These price increases occurred over a six-month period, not two. Second, Henry's equipment is badly out of date. In fact, we no longer market them. The cost of maintenance on old equipment naturally goes up because the cost of training new hires how to service these older machines has to be recovered by us from an ever-shrinking number of customers. Now what kind of response do you think we can make out of this situation?"

We answered quickly that telling Mr. Henry that his facts were wrong would be negative and argumentative and serve no positive purpose. Bob agreed. "O.K. So that's what you would NOT do. What WOULD you do?"

We made a guess. "Explain why his costs are so high?"

Bob just shook his head — sadly, we thought. "No, because that would mean I'd have to start my letter on a negative note. His equipment is essentially a Model T in today's market. If he doesn't know this, I'd be rubbing his nose in his ignorance. Once again I've got to say it's a good thing you guys aren't salesmen. You'd probably starve to death! Guess again. How can I start on a positive note?"

"Offer him some sort of a deal on new equipment?"

"Absolutely not!" Bob snapped. "He doesn't want to hear how he can spend money; he wants to hear how to save money! So I would begin by telling him how he can save money in the long run by listening to Fred Jones, our expert on the technology involved, who I was sending to visit with him and see if there is anything Henry could do to cut the rising cost of maintenance."

"Pretty clever," we said. "You get a complaint letter and figure out how to turn it into an invitation for someone to visit Henry and sell him new equipment."

"Not at all. That's just being cynical. I'm just accentuating the positive by letting him know how to keep from wasting a lot of money over the long run. Now, isn't that positive? To tell him in gory detail how he's in a hell of a mess with all that old, out-of-date equipment, is negative. I'm focusing on taking a positive step by having one of our best men look into Henry's problem and provide a remedy.

"After all, for all I know, there may be something that can be done to lower Henry's costs without buying new machines. It will simply be left up to Henry to decide to keep on paying the maintenance costs, which will constantly go up, or buy new equipment, whether it's ours or someone else's.

"And, furthermore, I would use a very personal style in the letter. And I'd show Henry that I appreciated the wittiness of his letter to me, by ending my letter to him with something like this: *I know that you will find Mr. Jones very helpful and knowledgeable. And I assure you, Mr. Henry, that I personally want to do everything possible to avoid having to play ping-pong, instead of golf.*"

Repaying Bob

Bob Gets Two Life Preservers

Our BLPLUS classes had been underway for some months and peace with the trainees reigned once more. Things also were going great in our relationship with Bob. He had stuck by us in our hard times. He had taught us everything he knew about effective business writing. He had even been the driving force behind our style investigations where both Bob and we learned things we had never known before. He had added much to our personal lives as well as to our careers. And we were grateful for any opportunity to offer some partial repayment for all he had done for us. Allow us, then, to end our book by relating two occasions where we had opportunities to assist him in two extremely difficult writing situations he faced.

In the first case, our assistance was admittedly indirect. It was our trainees in one of our BLPLUS classes who really came to Bob's rescue. In the second instance, which occurred late in our association, it was we who helped Bob, oddly enough, by pointing out to him that he had become so upset by a certain situation that he was not applying the very principles he had hammered into our heads.

83

FIRST CASE

One day, out of the blue, we got a call from Bob, summarily ordering us to his office, right away! No sooner had we entered his office than he jumped up from his chair and waved a letter under our noses.

"Look at this!" he shouted. He waved a piece of paper under our noses. "This letter was actually sent out, not only by this corporation, but by people handling management recruitment in my division! And not just sent to anyone, mind you, but to the nephew of Fred Harris!" We asked who Harris was. Bob's answer was bitter. "Very big customer of ours. Likes to throw his weight around. Not my first run-in with him. And now he sends me this!" Bob let us read the letter:

Dear Ms., Mrs., or Mr.,

Thank you for taking the time to interview with our recruiter on your campus.

We have processed your application.

Your qualifications, unfortunately, were not equal to those of other applicants. Therefore, we cannot offer you encouragement about possible employment by our corporation.

"The kid who received this is Harris's pet relative. Says he's like a son to him. The kid's close to graduation from college; so he applied for a job with us, and got this…you name it!…response. The kid then forwards this letter to his Uncle Fred who immediately hits the roof. So, naturally, since it came from my division, it's my personal fault! Harris sends it to me with a snotty message telling me what to do with the letter."

We said it was obviously an unfilled-out form letter mailed by mistake, never intended to be sent out as is. "What's the big deal?" we asked. "Obviously, just a careless mistake."

"That doesn't matter to Harris," Bob said. "Old No Mistakes Harris is his nickname."

"So what are you going to do?"

"I certainly am not going to fire whoever sent this out," Bob told us. "Know why? Because Harris demanded that I fire him. I wouldn't give Harris that satisfaction. But whoever wrote this is going to get his or her butt kicked, and good! And you're going to do the butt kicking for me." This did not sound appealing to us, but we kept quiet, a wise move when Bob was on a tear.

"I want you to put this letter in front of whichever's the sharpest section of your BLPLUS classes," Bob told us, "and ask the trainees what they think of it. And I'm going to sentence the guy who's responsible for this masterpiece to sit in the back of the class and listen to what the class has to say about it."

Exactly one week later, we noticed a strange young man sitting alone at a desk in the back of our classroom. We did not ask who he was or draw any attention to him. We put a transparency of his letter on the screen, gave the class an expurgated version of the true situation, and asked for their reactions. The trainees' comments were brutal:

----"Even the salutation is an insult. Imagine! Allowing the Ms., Mrs., Mr. to stay in the letter just rubs in the fact that this is obviously a form letter, and a lousy one at that. It shows how little the writer cares about making a favorable impression on the reader."

----"The first sentence is, I guess, supposed to buffer the effect of the 'no' that follows. But saying 'Thank you for taking the time…' is hardly positive. And it doesn't work. It's like writing some girl you dated just once and 'thanking her for taking the time' to go out with you."

----"That second paragraph, if it can be called that, is miserable — 'We have processed your application' is hardly a pleasantry. It would make me feel as if they'd put my application through a meat grinder!"

----"I especially hate the first sentence of the third paragraph. It offers him a gratuitous insult. He has asked for a job, not a disparagement of his relative qualifications."

----"The second sentence of the third paragraph is just as bad as the first sentence, if not worse. Not content with having already thoroughly insulted the young man, the next sentence hands him his head on a platter. It sounds as if they're telling him they would NEVER consider hiring him."

----"The closing sentence — 'we appreciate your interest in working with us' — is so phony, I can hardly believe it. Certainly the young man won't, that's for sure."

We challenged the trainees to break into groups and to rewrite this highly negative message in whatever style they thought would minimize the negative impact on the reader as much as possible. We paid no attention to the fact that the strange young man did not join any of the groups.

Two letters, quite different in every way, surfaced from the groups' efforts. Version I used a Personal style that the authors apparently believed would augment the positive tone of the letter, and blunt the impact of the negative message on the reader. Version II used essentially a Passive style in an attempt to make the negative news lower in impact and, hence, less hurtful to the reader.

Version I

Dear ---------:

During your interview on ---, you made such a fine impression on our recruiter that we wish we could offer you a position. But we cannot, simply because we do not have, at this time, enough openings to allow us to employ every student as qualified as you.

We congratulate you on your achievements while in college, and offer our very best wishes that you will soon find the ideal position, and enjoy a long and successful career.

Thank you for considering employment with us.

Version II

Dear ---------:

The time you spent interviewing with us on campus was much appreciated. Through such an in-depth interview, an opportunity to learn more about your career goals and interests was obtained.

The application you submitted has been reviewed with great interest, as were, of course, the applications of the many other fine graduates who interviewed with us.

As was explained during the interview, few openings are available at this time. And for each of these openings, there was literally an overwhelming number of applicants. Therefore, many strong candidates could not be encouraged.

We thank you, however, for giving us the chance to talk with you. And we wish you success in your future career.

The panel discussion showed that both revised versions were rated as being infinitely superior to the original. However, there was agreement on the fact that, despite Version I's dogged attempt to make something positive out of something completely negative, the ruse probably wouldn't work and might actually backfire. One trainee's opinion summed things up: "If I got this letter, I'd think, if they personally liked me that much, why didn't they make me an offer?" So much for the clever ruse! The group agreed that the more Version I was read, the less believable it would seem.

The Passive style of Version II, they felt, would be received the same in each rereading. One trainee summed up the group's conclusion about Version II. "At least, the reader won't think he's being handed a line."

We told Bob how the class had skewered the writer. He told us that our strange young man had reported to him immediately after the class and offered his resignation. "Did you accept it?" we asked. "Of course not! I told him he'd been punished enough already. But I did tell him that he had damn well better sign up for the BLPLUS course as fast as possible."

We showed Bob the two revised letters the groups had written. Then he said to us, in a sort of off-stage murmur, "Would you guys mind asking that class to check out ALL our form letters dealing with recruiting? I don't want to go through anything like this again. Believe me!"

We told him we would be only too glad to do so. We did not tell Bob, however, that a couple of people in the class had recognized the strange young man and put two and two together. On their own, they had helped him write a really terrific letter to Harris's nephew, confessing that he had accidentally sent him an unfinished, and completely inappropriate form letter. He apologized profusely and asked the nephew to please phone him if he would like to request a second interview. The nephew did call a day or so later. The strange young man told them that the nephew just laughed at the notion of a second interview, saying, "Hell, no! I only agreed to interview at all because my Uncle Fred insisted on it." He then went on to state that he had no interest whatsoever in a business career, and that he had great confidence in the ultimate success of the rock band he had formed during his college years.

Bob never heard another word about it from Fred Harris.

SECOND CASE

In this instance, we, not our trainees, had the opportunity to help Bob. This is the best case Bob ever brought us, but we never used it in any of our classes, for reasons that will soon be obvious.

We want to share it here, at the end of our book, because this case requires a writer to put into practice everything that we learned from Bob over the many years. And, oddly enough, Bob was so distraught by the situation that he simply wasn't thinking straight, and we had to pitch in and help him handle a most distressing personal situation.

* * * * * * * * * * *

One day, Bob came into our office, looking disturbed. After he had taken a seat, he said, "You know, the hardest thing I have to do is fire someone who's done a good job." He raised a palm to head off any questions. "I know you're wondering why anybody would let someone go if they're doing a good job. Well, it happens all the time in business. Things change and some good people get caught by the changes."

He went on to tell us about a man we'll call "Larry." Three years ago, Bob had brought Larry into his division to head what they called Vulcan, a highly technical research project in Larry's area of expertise. Larry had been signed to a length-of-the-project contract. Results over the first two and a half years had been minimal, and costs were high. The corporate Board of Directors had decided to discontinue funding the project; so, Bob had no choice but to let Larry go.

"It's very awkward for me," Bob said. "He's an internationally recognized scientist, for one thing. He's a very fine person, to boot. I've talked with Larry, of course, about the budgetary concerns, and no one knows better than he that the results have been lousy to date. But I'm sure he's not expecting the axe to fall, at least not so quickly. There are some contractual complications that I don't have to concern myself about. But I'm the guy who has to write the letter of dismissal. This means, of course, that both the Board and our legal people will get copies of my letter to him.

"So, I'm caught between my personal regard for Larry, professional respect for a fine scientist, and my corporate responsibility. Damn it! This is the most painful letter I've ever had to write. His wife and mine have become friends, and Larry and I have always been close." He reached into his pocket and pulled out a draft of his letter. "I want to know what you think of it." Here is what Bob had written:

Dear Larry,

No one realizes more than I do the tremendous amount of time and effort you put into attempting to make the Vulcan Project viable. All of us in the company sincerely hoped that this project would prove successful and that matters would work out differently from the way they have.

Even though we have the greatest respect for your energy and dedication, I have the unfortunate responsibility to inform you that the project will be discontinued at the end of this year, and that there will be no further need for your services.

Let me assure you, Larry, that we regret this decision, no one more than I. You can be sure that we will give you the highest of personal recommendations and will do everything in our power to help you relocate. We sincerely regret that we have to take this action. And we regret the personal disappointment and inconvenience it causes you and your family.

We sat for a minute or so, thinking. It was obvious that Bob tried to apply the principles of BLPLUS rather than just plain BLing. He had wisely not BLed the negative message, but had attempted to bury the bad news in the second paragraph.

We instantly focused our attention on a very critical fault in Bob's draft. His use of a personal style was potentially lethal in an extremely negative message like this. We told him so and he immediately objected. "What's wrong with my use of a personal style? I used it deliberately to soften the bad news, to make it sound not so cold and impersonal."

"Wait, Bob. We're not implying you don't care. We are simply afraid that being as personal as you are in this draft will boomerang in a situation so very negative as this. We're thinking about how your friend Larry might very well react. We both strongly question whether the message might not be far better received if it were decidedly less personal in style."

Bob shook his head. "I don't understand. How could it be less painful to Larry if it were less personal?"

"Discover for yourself. Play the part of Larry. Try to imagine what Larry feels at the very moment he finishes reading the letter for the first time. How do you think you would feel, if you really were Larry?"

Bob answered without hesitation. "I'd be stunned! And I'd be hurt, badly hurt."

"Yes, you would. So continue to play the part of Larry, sitting at home, hurt. What do you think you'd do next?"

"I imagine I'd read the letter several more times."

"And?"

"I guess I'd get madder and more defensive each time," Bob replied.

"Absolutely! And with each reading, you would change. By the second reading, at most, you wouldn't be the same old friend Larry." Bob said nothing. We continued, "Don't you agree that this new, angry, hurt Larry might be extremely suspicious of your well-intentioned friendliness that is in stark contrast to the fact that you've just fired him?"

"What are you getting at?" Bob demanded. "Are you saying that I'm insincere?"

"Not you. It's the Personal style that's causing the trouble."

"What in the world are you talking about?" Bob demanded.

"We're getting you upset. And at a bad time. We're sorry," we told him. "Why don't we take this up some time later?"

"Hell, no!" Bob shouted. "I've got to get this letter off to Larry as soon as possible — and to the Board also."

"All right, Bob," we said. "We'll keep going, if that's what you want. Maybe we can think it through together." Bob nodded.

"First of all, this case is remarkably complex. I don't think we've ever dealt with something like it before. A strongly negative message situation where someone has to write a letter which is going to be read by two different readers — two readers with completely opposing viewpoints — Larry's and the Board's. And both readers are actually UP. The Board, obviously, but Larry is also UP because of your friendship with him.

"You have to write a letter that the Board will examine very carefully. Obviously, you don't want anything you write to Larry to cause trouble for you with the Board. Judging from what you tell us, the Board doesn't give a damn about Larry's feelings. They just want the project over and done with and Larry gone. You, on the other hand, want Larry to know that you, personally, are truly sorry to be the one who has to deliver the bad news. So you fall back on a personal style of writing that seems warm and close. And now you can't accept our opinion that a personal style will boomerang in this case.

"You know we've done a lot of research, which you've supported royally, to find out which styles work best in which situations. And we have found out, beyond any reasonable doubt, that the use of an intensely personal style is usually poisonous in a strongly negative message situation like this one."

Bob seemed sulky. "I don't see what's wrong with my using a personal style. I used it deliberately to soften the bad news — to make it sound less cold and impersonal. And it does. You can't deny it!"

"Bob, we're not denying anything. We just know that this version will not accomplish your goals with either audience, neither with the Board nor with Larry!"

"Right now, I say the hell with whether the Board likes the letter. I just care about Larry's feelings. That's why I used a personal style and, by God, I still think it's the right thing to do. I don't care how much research you've done."

"Look," we said, "give us a chance to prove that what you've written to Larry will be disastrous."

"Go ahead and try. Prove it!"

"All right, we will. But you've got to keep in mind that this letter is going to two very different readers. What pleases one may displease the other. Let's go through your proposed letter, line by line, and consider how each line will go over with both of your readers. But while we do, please remember that just five minutes ago, you said that your old pal, Larry, who reads your letter for the first time, will not be the same old pal Larry who reads it for the last time. He'll undoubtedly be a hurt, angry, and insulted ex-old pal, at least for a while."

Bob nodded. "I remember. But what's that got to do with a personal style being so wrong? You'll have to show me."

"Sure," we agreed. "Pretend you are the Larry who is reading the letter for the fifth time. He's hurt and really very angry by now. He's out for blood. He takes one more look at the first sentence. Perhaps he reads it aloud: *'No one realizes more than I do the tremendous work and effort you put into attempting to make the Vulcan project viable.'* How might this hurt and angry Larry react to that opening on a fifth reading? Can't you imagine him muttering, 'If my old friend, Bob, truly realized how hard I worked, why did he turn against me and cancel the project?'"

Bob exploded. "What do you want me to say? That the Board overruled me? You know damn well I couldn't put that in writing!"

"Well, that's exactly what you are actually implying. Let us show how the personal style you use to soothe Larry will get you in trouble with the Board. Look at what you say in your second paragraph: '*...I have the unfortunate responsibility to inform you that the project will be discontinued by the end of this year, and that there will be no further need for your services.'* If you were on the Board and glad to be rid of Larry, what would you read into your telling Larry that you have '...the UNFORTUNATE responsibility...' for firing him? We don't think they would like that wording. They probably would read into those words the strong suggestion being made to Larry that firing him was not your idea. Not good, Bob. And Larry wouldn't like it either. This hurt, angry Larry will think the word 'unfortunate' is sheer baloney."

Bob was starting to steam. We thought it wise to hurry along. "Now take a look at the third paragraph: *'Let me assure you, Larry, that we regret this decision, no one more than I.'* This is a half-truth, Bob, and you know it. YOU regret the decision! There is no WE about it. The Board does not regret it a bit. In your desire to minimize the hurt to Larry's feelings, you are doing exactly what you have always hated most. Not 'telling it like it is,' and relying instead on what will, under the circumstances, be regarded by Larry as a bunch of BS, instead of a half-truth you can't openly express. Furthermore, it is BS that will boomerang with your old friend, Larry, because he's so shocked and hurt that he will probably be ready to brand your 'I'm so sorry' statements as mere crocodile tears."

Bob was looking pretty green around the gills, but we had to finish what we started. "And what about the last sentence of the draft...? *'And we regret the personal disappointment and inconvenience it causes you and your family.'* How do you think this will go over with an angry, hurt Larry?"

Now Bob was looking even greener. He was starting to "get it" and he didn't like it at all. "Oh, my God!" Bob said. "'My family!' That's what Larry will think. 'And I've only been thinking of myself. What a shock this is going to be to my wife. And what about my kids in school? It means moving and financial problems.'"

Bob paused, so we took a deep breath and finished up. "In a nutshell, here's what an angry Larry will conclude — that you and your whole company don't care a damn about him, his family, or all the hard work he has put in! And because you are the one who is actually firing him, he won't react favorably at all to your warm, personal statements. You said to us that you wanted to sound close and caring to Larry. But in a situation like this, it simply will not work!"

Bob sat, looking much as if we had just hit him over the head with a baseball bat. After he mulled it over for a minute or two, he managed a wry smile. "And, other than that, Mrs. Lincoln, how did you like the play? All right, I give up. What do I do? Shoot all the personal pronouns?"

"Just about. Let's try writing it in the Impersonal style, without any I's or we's." We went to our keyboard. Here is what we put together:

Dear Larry,

The tremendous amount of time and effort you put into attempting to make the Vulcan project viable is widely recognized. It was sincerely hoped that this project would prove successful and that matters would have turned out differently from the way they have.

While there is the greatest respect for your energy and dedication, the decision has been made to discontinue the project by the end of this year. Therefore, there will be no further need for your services.

This decision is unfortunate. The highest of personal recommendations will be gladly given, and everything possible will be done to facilitate your relocation.

"What do you think?" we asked.

"I don't like it." Bob snapped. "In fact, I hate it! It's not only Impersonal, it's Passive!"

"We don't like it, either," we told him. "But it doesn't matter whether YOU or WE like it or not. It doesn't even matter how well it goes over with Larry. He gets the letter and reads through it for the first time. Then he reads it again and again several times. No matter how many times he reads it, he will never like it, but the letter's impersonal and passive style will exhibit the same 'blah' tone it had on its first reading.

"Sure, it's dull and as impersonal as a training manual, but it doesn't give Larry the feeling that you are trying to con him. This version delivers the bad news in a flat, businesslike way. It leaves you, Bob, as an individual, out of the situation. Moreover, it does not accidentally drag Larry's wife and family into the picture. It doesn't shed a drop of what Larry, justly feeling sorry for himself, probably will be quick to characterize as crocodile tears.

"We know what disturbs you. It's because this version is so businesslike and seemingly cold and impersonal, you fear it will be resented by Larry. You told us the Board would see a copy of what you sent Larry. Well, the Board would have hated your first draft. They'd have thought, rightly, that it made them look like the bad guys, which of course they are. But this version will go over fine with the Board, we're sure. So give it to them. It does the job you were forced to do, and won't irritate them."

Bob stared at us, unable to believe we were actually saying these hurtful things.

"Let us remind you of some of the things you have taught us. You taught us that being known for honesty and sincerity was the key to successful communication. But you also reminded us that most letters contain more than one message, and in a strongly negative situation, we should always try to find a way to keep the focus on whatever is positive, if only faintly so, instead of on the negative. So, ask yourself this. What's the only positive message possible in this miserable situation?"

Bob was quick to answer. "It's that I promise to do all I can to help him relocate."

"Right!" we said. "There's nothing stopping you from doing what you can for Larry behind the scenes to help him relocate. And there's something else you taught us that you should remember and apply to this case. It was that there are some situations which are so negative that you should do everything possible to avoid having to put anything in writing. Well, doesn't this case qualify?"

"Sure it does, but I'm being forced to... The Board...," Bob stopped suddenly. He looked up. "I'll be damned! I see what you're getting at. I visit with Larry. I hand him the letter and tell him to read it later. Face to face, I tell him about the decision. I talk about everything I'm going to do to help him relocate. I tell him I'm really sorry, but I leave the Board out of it, as much as possible so that no one can claim I dumped the blame on the Board while I weaseled out."

"That's right," we said, "and when he reads your letter later, it won't matter a bit the way it is phrased. It won't matter. He'll know without your telling him that it was written for the Board, because you have told him personally that you will help him."

Bob took a long look at us. "So now you are able to quote me against myself. And, moreover, make it stick!" He paused for a moment; then he smiled and put out his hand. "You know, I'm really surprised at how much I'm supposed to have taught you guys about smart writing without apparently learning a damn thing myself!" He shook our hands. "Thanks for helping with this. I mean it!" And, knowing Bob, he did.

Bob's Rules Applied to Winning the War

Closing the Floodgates

The BLPLUS course continued to be a hit with management trainees. We taught it to excellent reviews for several more years. Then, as we mentioned earlier, changes in both Bob's and our lives led to the end of our working together.

Bob's final assignment for us was to create Exhibit B, what Bob called a "simple" chart which would summarize everything we had learned: first, about BLing, and then, about using BLPLUS to write more sensitively when such was wise. The creation of this not-so-simple chart not only wrapped up everything we had learned in working with him over two decades; it also wrapped up our longest-running consulting assignment.

We end this book as we started, remembering the farewell lunch Bob threw us, and the solemn promise we had made to declare war on bad e-mail writing if ever the day came that e-mail, despite its speed and convenience, had produced a flood that was wasting more people's time and company's money than ever before in history. That era has clearly arrived.

In fact, the problem is still growing. *USA Today* (July 24, 2003) stated that "An estimated 11 billion e-mails are sent each day worldwide, triple the level of 1999." How many of these 11 billion e-mail messages could pass Bob's "So What?" test? Very few, apparently, since the *USA Today* report devotes considerable space to describing how many busy executives are hiring assistants to filter out the few e-mails that are worthy of their boss's time. But adding assistants just adds to an organization's communication costs.

Who today is doing something about shrinking time and costs by teaching writers to follow Bob's Rules? Nobody, of course. Before this book, what would today's top executives have had to do? Re-invent Bob's Rules? Hardly likely. It took Bob and us 20 years to come up with what is summarized in Bob's "simple" chart.

We are glad that we have lived long enough to write this chronicle of the development of Bob's Rules for efficient, effective and successful business writing. Finishing this book and making it available to you and other readers is the only way we knew of to spread Bob's Rules to keep our promise to Bob. Now it's up to you and all other readers to help win this war in the nation's corporate trenches. You carry our best hopes and wishes with you.

EXHIBIT B. BOB'S BLPLUS RULES FOR SENSITIVE MESSAGES

A. POSITIVE MESSAGES

"Good news" types of positive messages are, by far, the easiest of all sensitive communications to write. It does not matter whether they are sent UP or DOWN, INSIDE or OUTSIDE.

Organizational choice: BL! Why not? Nobody ever gets upset about receiving good news, so why bury it?

Style choice: Forceful and Personal styles strongly preferred by readers. ("I'm darned glad you got the promotion! You deserve it!")

B. NEGATIVE MESSAGES

Negative messages, obviously, are highly sensitive. Nobody likes to get bad news, or to be criticized, rejected, or turned down. Strongly hostile reader reactions can result, especially when the message is sent UP — either INSIDE or OUTSIDE.

NEGATIVE UP — INSIDE:

Organizational choice: Whether negative messages sent UP inside your company can safely be BLed depends upon the writer's personal relationship with the reader.

Style choice: BLPLUS makes it possible to BL all but the most personally offensive messages. To minimize such a message's impact on your reader, use either the Passive style, or a combination of the Passive and Impersonal styles.

NEGATIVE UP — OUTSIDE:

Organizational choice: BLing a negative message UP to, say, your company's biggest customer seems, on the face of it, generally inadvisable, unless the writer enjoys a close personal relationship with the reader. Do <u>not</u> BL a blatantly negative message. Present one of the other more reader-friendly messages first — such as, "*It certainly was great to see you again last week and to hear that your company is doing so well. However, with regard to your suggestion that we lower our prices on...I need to explain that circumstances, at present, do not allow...*" (If there is no somewhat positive message available, consider making one up!)

Style choice: Use either the Passive style or a combination of the Passive and Impersonal styles.

NEGATIVE DOWN — INSIDE:

Organizational choice: In many of today's businesses, where strict "Control and Command" is no longer the rule, negative messages sent DOWN must be tactful. Each writer must decide whether it is wise to BL the negative message, or tactfully to prepare the reader for the bad news before delivering it.

Style choice: Regardless of whether the negative message is BLed, or is buried in the middle paragraph of the letter, its impact can — or should — be lessened by use of a mixture of the Impersonal and the Passive styles.

NEGATIVE DOWN — OUTSIDE:

Organizational choice: Even in a situation where you are the "biggest customer" and the reader is the supplier, careful consideration should be given before BLing a strongly negative message.

Style choice: Both the Forceful and the Personal styles should be avoided in such messages. Impersonal and Passive styles should be used in most instances.

C. PERSUASIVE MESSAGES

POSITIVE PERSUASIVE: Those which ask readers to take an action that is clearly in their own best interests. ("Get your flu shot today!")

Organizational choice: BL! Why not?

Style choice: Both the Forceful and the Personal styles are strongly recommended as complements to a positive-persuasive message.

NEGATIVE PERSUASIVE: Those which ask readers (a) to take an action in which they see absolutely no personal benefit, or (b) to alter or abandon an opinion they hold dear and accept one that contradicts that opinion.

Organizational choice: BL! Such forthrightness demonstrates strong personal belief in the value to readers of doing what is asked of them.

Style choice: Personal and Forceful. A Passive or Impersonal style will be perceived subliminally by readers as weak and unpersuasive, demonstrating the writer's lack of confidence in what is being asked of the reader.

HOW TO APPLY BOB'S BLPLUS RULES

In Bob's estimation, 90% of all messages that people write in their career are so routine and harmless that there is no reason in the world NOT to BL them! (See Exhibit A, page 27) In the other 10%, there may be critically important sensitive messages that, if handled well, will markedly advance your career. And there also may well be a few really touchy messages in that 10% that, if handled poorly, may serve to damage your career severely. So be careful! Bob's BLPLUS rules can help you think through what you need to do to be successful in dealing with all types of message situations.

Imagine that you are sitting at your keyboard, trying to decide how best to handle just such a delicate writing task, one that requires careful thought in order to develop a successful message strategy. You must always keep in mind that letters, memos or reports, especially lengthy ones, usually contain SEVERAL messages. Your task is to consider carefully HOW your reader will react to each message. It is vitally important that you constantly keep in mind that the advice given in Bob's BLPLUS rules applies to each separate message in the proposed communication.

Bob's recommendations as to organization and style will (or can) be different for each message included in a particular communication. If one of your communication's messages is positive, follow the advice given for positive messages. If another message will be seen by the reader as negative, follow the advice given for negative messages.

Exhibit B will serve as your guide, but only after YOU have done some sound preliminary thinking, and have answered each of the following questions:

    1. How many messages are involved in your proposed communication? Which of these messages will produce the greatest IMPACT on the reader? If, for example, this high-impact message is "strongly negative," look under NEGATIVE MESSAGES in Exhibit B. If that most important message is "strongly positive," then refer to POSITIVE MESSAGES in the Exhibit. If your proposed letter contains a mixture of both positive and negative messages, remember that it is always better to high impact the positive message(s). But you must use

your best judgment as to which positive message should be presented first, which last and exactly where the "bad news" should be presented.

2. Take into consideration the direction in which the messages will be sent (UP or DOWN, INSIDE or OUTSIDE). In a sensitive communication, direction often makes a significant difference in how delicate submessages should be organized, and which style is wisest to use. Notice that Exhibit B's advice on negative letters differs when UP or DOWN and INSIDE or OUTSIDE are taken into consideration.

3. Before you settle on a definite plan in any highly important and strongly negative message situation, you must consider whether there are unique, perhaps personal, issues that should be taken into account. Answer the following questions:
    (a) How will your reader react to the fact that YOU are the one who is presenting these messages?
    (b) What is your personal relationship and reputation with the reader?
    (c) What is your organization's standing with the reader?

4. When planning how best to handle an extremely sensitive, highly negative message situation, such as one written UP to a powerful reader, SLOW DOWN. Print out a draft of your proposed letter. If that draft seems to you to have even the slightest possibility of causing a strongly negative reaction in the reader, don't send it. Sleep on it. Then later, with a fresh eye, consider how your reader will react to what you have written, and whether the tone resulting from your choice of organizational pattern and writing style is one that will likely achieve success. If such is not the case, go back to Question 1, and try again.

5. If the end result of all your efforts is that no combination of organization, style and order of presentation seems effective, don't write! Consider whether a different medium of communication might have a better chance of, if not success, then a significantly decreased chance of creating a total debacle. What is contained in Bob's BLPLUS rules can help greatly, but it cannot advise you on how to do the impossible.